THE AUDACITY TO LEAD

Sybil F. Dunwoody

Sybil F. Dunwoody

Dedication

I dedicate this book to my parents, the late Elder James and Carolyn Viola Darby, my true inspirations and the head cheerleaders of my greater cloud of witnesses; the absolute best parents anyone could ever ask for. Their teaching, discipline and love made me a strong woman. As a result, I'm able to stand boldly on the prayers and sacrifices they made.

In addition, I acknowledge those who were influential in my ability to lead, which include all of my children, both natural and spiritual. God has blessed me with children from all walks of life and various backgrounds that call me pastor, mother, auntie and friend.

I must also make mention of my brother James, a loyal co-laborer of the gospel, who supports me from a distance but is always there when I need him.

Also, I would like to thank a host of friends both in and out of ministry. Together with my church family, this support team has helped mold me into the leader I am today.

Finally, I would like to thank my spiritual son in the gospel, Richard Carrington, for helping me bring my journey to life on the pages of this book.

Sybil F. Dunwoody

"Be shepherds of God's flock that is under your care, watching over them — not because you must, but because you are willing, as God wants you to be; not pursuing dishonest gain, but eager to serve."
—*1 Peter 5:2*

Contents

Preface   2

Chapter

1	When The Lord Chooses You	6
2	He Is No Respecter of Persons	15
3	It Doesn't Matter What They Think	31
4	Your Gift Will Make Room For You	35
5	Preparation For The Journey	47
6	My Role Model	60
7	A Hard Lesson Learned	67
8	When You Think The Unthinkable	76
9	Moving On	85
10	Organizing The Right Team	100
11	Sometimes They Leave	114
12	We Are Just The Vessels	120
13	Delivered From Dogma And Dysfunction	130
14	My Commitment To The Whosoevers	142
15	Transforming Churchgoers To Kingdom Members	154
16	The Lord Will Give You A Name Change	160

Preface

I am favored to have been blessed with wonderful, God-fearing parents who provided me with a strong foundation that was rooted in the Word and Will of God. My parents demanded uncompromising integrity, coupled with a spirit of excellence and anything less was unacceptable. Their strong belief and commitment to holiness and faith provided a living example that all things were possible when you not only believe but truly live for God. One of my mother's favorite scripture passages was: *"Follow peace with all men, and holiness, without which no man shall see the Lord." —Hebrews 12:14*. Although my mother has been gone for some time now, I can still hear her quote that scripture in my spirit as if she was with me in service.

My parents lived a life of integrity that was authentic, holy and uncompromising. Notwithstanding, they were not perfect and never professed to be, but rather defined themselves as sinners saved by grace. Furthermore, they believed holiness (the act of living holy) was a lifestyle choice rather than a religious denomination or affiliation.

The type of holiness they lived was a holistic approach which spread into every area of your life. From an early age, my parents instilled in me the passion and commitment to serve God. They informed me that if I walked upright, kept a repenting heart and constantly worked to strengthen my relationship with God, He would guide my path and protect me from all manner of evil in whatever form it appeared. They reassured me that everything I committed unto the Lord, He would establish my plans, so I committed my whole life unto Him.

Given the relationship I developed with Christ over time, I soon realized I was not the one in complete control of my destiny. Although I had big plans and breathtaking dreams for my life and even made proper preparations, they all had to line up with His will and purpose for my life, otherwise, they were for not.

Therefore, I deferred my will to His plan, letting His word lead me. Quickly I adopted the psalmist David's declaration, *"Your Word is a lamp to my feet, and a light to my path." —Psalm 119:1.* Till this day, I live that scripture daily, and because of it, my life of service and faithfulness to the Most High God has been astounding. I have been blessed to see the world and do things I only dreamed of as a little girl. My obedience and ability to surrender to God's will empowered me and gave me favor, much more than I desired and even more than I deserved.

As a result, I wrote this book to encourage all and share my astonishing journey with those who have accepted God's call to ministry work. I am a strong woman, a yielded vessel who understands that apart from God, I'm nothing. My story is meant to uplift those new to ministry work and others in the midst of ministry work, contemplating their next move.

Leadership in any capacity is tough and motivating people to rally around your vision is even tougher. I encourage you to hang in there and hold fast to God's Word. *"Though it tarries, wait for it." —Habakkuk 2:3.* It's essential to realize that this often travelled road has imperfections and bumps along the way. There is no such thing as a walk on easy street with Christ. It is critical to remember God dwells (resides and lives) within you. Given that premise, you have all the strength and power to reach and fulfill your vision — even take it beyond.

I didn't choose God or my present office of Pastor, God chose me before the foundation of the world. In doing so, He also equipped me for this incredible journey. My acceptance of the call to ministry constituted a paradigm shift that many in my circles were not ready for, however, one which was preordained. God's calling represented a divine assignment that no secret back room deal could overrule and no antiquated system could hinder. Therefore, be encouraged knowing that if God be for you, He is more than the world against you. —*Romans 8:31*

One

When The Lord Chooses You

"Stand fast therefore in the liberty wherewith Christ hath made us free, and be not entangled again with the yoke of bondage."
—Galatians 5:1

Over the last twenty-five years, I have learned a few valuable lessons concerning ministry and service in the Kingdom of God. Lesson One: God has a work and a position for each of us who serve Him. God doesn't have what some call "bench members." Once you commit to the Lord, your life of service begins. A common saying is that we were "saved to serve," not "saved to sit." Lesson Two: God is no respecter of persons. What He does for others, He can do for you. It doesn't matter where you started, what your lineage is or what awful acts you may have participated in or committed in the past. Lesson Three: God decides who is most capable of doing a work for Him. No man, no institutions and no antiquated systems decide who will do a work for God.

No matter what you have been through, God can still use you.

Accepting those three principles will make your work with the Lord empowering. The bottom line is that we are vessels to be used for His glory. So often, people who have been redeemed, whose lives have been transformed by the renewing of their mind, still possess some skepticism when it comes to working for the Lord. While they have repented for their sins and have been blood-washed, they choose to carry guilt and shame, which causes them to feel unworthy and inadequate to meet the criteria for ministry work in the Kingdom of God.

Some believe that past indiscretions, current struggles and mistakes have disqualified them for Kingdom work. Not that we should feel high-minded, none of us are worthy except the Father God. However, through grace, the unmerited favor of a loving God, we become eligible to be used for His glory. As yielded vessels, He decides what capacity He will use us. The Apostle Paul wrote in the book of Ephesians: *"And He gave some as apostles, and some as prophets, and some as evangelists, and some as pastors and teachers, for the equipping of the saints for the work of service, to the building up of the body of*

Christ." —*Ephesians 4:11-12*. Therefore, letting us know that we all play a part in His plan for our salvation. Although we have separate and distinct functions, collectively our calling is to build up the body of Christ, while forcefully advancing the Kingdom.

The enemy hates that we have been chosen by God. As a result, the enemy, our adversary, in his cunning ways uses our weaknesses and vulnerabilities to hold us down and hinder our work. Because the enemy is a spirit and ruler of this world, he knows our flaws, struggles and innermost secrets. He uses that combined knowledge hoping to discourage us to the point that we doubt God and His calling on our lives. The enemy is the chief discourager and deceiver of the brethren. Today he is more sophisticated and subtle but remains steadfast looking for angles and opportunities to get the saints out of fellowship with the Lord. The Apostle Peter describes him as a roaring lion seeking whom he can devour.

As a result, I am quick to remind the people of God that we live in a depraved world and none of us are free from flaws. All of us are or were marred vessels that need or needed restoration by Jesus, our Savior. The great King David, the psalmist, declared: *"Behold, I was shapen in iniquity; and in sin did my mother conceive me."* — *Psalm 51:5*.

We are all works in progress who struggle to keep our flesh under subjection and repent for our sins. None of us can say we are without sin. John the Apostle stated: *"If we say that we have no sin, we deceive ourselves, and the truth is not in us."* —*1 John 1:6*. None of us have arrived, and all of us fall short.

One of the adversary's greatest feats is the delusion of making us think we are okay in our sins. All sin must be repented and it's a daily, hourly, and in some instances, a minute-by-minute process. Sin unrepented and ignored, either willfully or unintentionally, grows and festers like a malignant cancer.

Many of us, in moments of arrogance, weakness and ignorance, have done deeds in the past of which we are not so proud. These deeds were completely contrary to living a life for Christ. Some of our daily struggles are so disconcerting that many of us are holding on to our salvation by a thread. And as Christ's impending return draws nearer, it is necessary for Him to shorten the days. In fact, the Bible lets us know that if He does not, no flesh will be saved.

While some of our life stories or prior lives before salvation are more riveting than others, all represent the shortcomings and often the depravity of man. We all have a story to tell and a history on record. As I have matured and seen more of life, nothing really surprises me. I know in the final analysis, man has feet of clay and is subject to fall at any given moment. And over the years, I have seen many of those rises and fallings, up close and personal.

Many people can attest to what they regard as being on the top shelf of life one moment and suddenly at rock bottom the next. And the collapse can either be swift or it can be a slow, tedious, torturous decline. Either way, it's humbling and sometimes fatal — not only in our walk with Christ but even in our natural lives. Turn on the television or search the internet today and see preachers dropping dead in the pulpit because of sin and disobedience. People are turning their backs on God and deciding to pursue alternative lifestyles. People that were once perceived to be Christian stalwarts are turning their backs on Christ at alarming rates.

Some people experience such severe hurts and losses that they simply give up on God, blaming Him for their troubles. Fortunately, some come back to their senses, while others wander aimlessly in the wilderness of life, never reaching their promise land or place of fulfillment while on earth. However, I'm ever mindful to let those with whom I have the privilege to pastor and mentor know that we all are susceptible to falling — for we are all just flesh. Flesh is never perfect and is always flawed. The Bible states that: *"We know that none are perfect or good but the Father our God." —Romans 3:10.* The Apostle Paul in his writing in the Book of Romans lets us know that, *"For all have sinned, and come short of the glory of God." —Romans 3:23.*

Nevertheless, the great God we serve saved us for such a time as this. Therefore, it is our responsibility to possess the mustard seed faith and work diligently in the capacity and vocation which we have been called. This means living a life of integrity and excellence, whereas we have been called out of darkness and into the marvelous light.

It is incumbent upon us as ministers of the gospel to tell the world the Good News of Jesus Christ and help empower the captive to become free. There is nothing we can do about the past. The past is simply the past, a closed chapter or chapters of our lives. We acknowledge it, we learn from it and we build upon the good, while shunning the bad. But what is imperative is that we don't dwell, romanticize or repeat our past sinful lives.

Remember God calls us simply because He wants to. He doesn't necessarily call us because we have superhuman faith; nor does He call us because we dot every "i" and cross every "t." Neither does He call us because we are in some perceived chosen denomination, and we believe God speaks to our group more than others. So many think they have a lock on heaven and their way is the only way. That type of closed-minded thinking has led many people astray.

The Lord will use whom He sees fit when and in whatever capacity He chooses. Therefore, we the called of Christ need to possess a repenting heart and the intestinal fortitude to stand ready and willing to do the work of the Lord, regardless of what it calls for. By "stand," I mean being present in the moment and being the loyal and faithful soldier that God has called us to be. And there will be times we have to stand even when we don't want to. We have to stand when we feel like giving up and even when we are all alone. However, when we stand for the Lord, we position ourselves to advance the Kingdom of God.

Consequently, today with the onslaught of social media websites and the information highway overload, one inappropriate posting or picture can disqualify you for a job or certain career. With Facebook and all of the other sites out there on the world-wide-web, many of our lives are open books. There is no hiding or living in secret. With one click of a mouse, your whole life is visible to millions of people. Today, employers conduct background checks to see what you are saying online, and more importantly, what is being said about you.

All that we are involved with is public knowledge. We could miss out on a job opportunity because someone may have posted something negative or unfavorable about us that may not even be true but is out there on the internet posing as fact. The landscape of the world has changed drastically from just a generation ago. But be not dismayed, the "all knowing" and "all wise" God is aware of everything we were, are and will become.

He knew our destiny and future before we were even conceived. The omniscient One determines who will work for Him at the most important job in the

Kingdom of God; which is that of a servant. And when He chooses you, simply be open, accept the calling and be malleable to the qualifying. Fret not because of past troubles or take no confidence in past successes or current status in the natural life.

One of my goals in writing this book is to let everyone know that you can accomplish anything in life if the Lord goes with you. The Apostle Paul summed it up best in his letter to the Romans: *"What then shall we say to these things? If God is for us, who can be against us?"* — *Romans 8:31.* What an empowering declaration!

So, to all who are ready to start your journey in ministry or if you are renewing your commitment to advancing the Kingdom of God, there is room for you at the table. Come forth my brother and sister, together we can be God's change agents for a lost and suffering world.

Two

He Is No Respecter Of Persons

Then Peter opened his mouth, and said, "Of a truth I perceive that God is no respecter of persons..." —Acts 10:34

I like to think that I'm unique in many ways. When I accepted the call to serve in ministry as a pastor, I didn't have a disreputable past, nor was I ever in any legal or ethical trouble. People in the church circles were familiar to me and my family. I wasn't one you would call a troublemaker or someone that operated contrary in ministry by any stretch of the imagination. So I was prayerful that my transition to leadership would be somewhat smooth. However, that was far from the reality. The truth is there was huge opposition to my appointment but not for any actions I committed. Believe it or not, my transgression was being a loyal and faithful member of a church body and having the temerity to accept the call at a time and in an organization that wasn't exactly glad to have me as a member in the capacity of pastor. God didn't have a problem with me because He chose and anointed me. It was the church denomination who had a problem with my leading.

It's important to note that regardless of the organization's stand on women preachers, I'm a proud, card-carrying member of the grand ole Church of God in Christ, a denomination with more than 6 million members and one of the largest Pentecostal assemblies. Nevertheless, with all of its rich traditions and great works, it's a brotherhood that doesn't accept women in the role of pastor. So I'm left to operate in a paradoxical relationship. Furthermore, I don't believe the church's stance on women makes it all bad or negate the great works it does. However, it does put the church body at a disadvantage, whereas we are living in what many church theologians deem as the last days — the time the prophet Joel spoke of: *"And afterward, I will pour out my Spirit on all people. Your sons and daughters will prophesy, your old men will dream dreams, your young men will see visions." — Joel 2:28.*

As we sit poised to possibly elect the first woman president of the United States, our church has some catching up to do. Today, women run a large percentage of some of the most successful Fortune 500 companies. They are leading countries and governments around the world. Women outnumber men in the church and in the workforce. Today 80 percent of women have to work for households to function economically. Long gone are the days of barefoot and pregnant when women stayed at home waiting hand and foot on their husbands. In spite of how far we have come, I didn't set out to challenge the church's stance, because I had no desire to be pastor or seek any leadership position; but the Lord saw differently. Originally, His plans were not my plans so the church's archaic ways of thinking really didn't affect me in my day-to-day walk with Christ.

I knew there were women leading churches, but I had no real opinion about it. However, when the Lord elevated and promoted me to pastor, it was then that the issue came smack dab in my face, causing me to deal with the outdated thinking of the day. I could not let the tenets of the denomination, no matter how hallowed we believed they were, dictate my assignment from God. My assignment was bigger than the church protocol.

Nevertheless, let me be clear, I have and always will love my church and the denomination in which I serve, in spite of any policies that I may disagree with. I serve with honor and integrity and am totally committed to making it a more effective organization. There are some traditions and practices that need to be addressed and changed. However, I'm not that shortsighted to think at my command everything must change to suit me. With that being said, change is a process and it takes time. One thing my dad always told me was: "Sybil, you don't throw the baby out with the bath water." He let me know that no organization, job or person was perfect. It's in your best interest to look for the good in all. In life we are not going to agree with everyone 100 percent of the time, but as long as we are on the same page philosophically then we can work together. Truly, I was willing to work with anyone who was living a life of integrity and focused on advancing the Kingdom of God.

However, sometimes that's easier said than done, especially when you believe that some of the same people who profess to be allied with you may be placing stumbling blocks in your way. Enduring this process, I learned there were a lot of people that said one thing and did another; claimed to support me and be a friend privately but acted totally contrary in public and official settings. It was utter hypocrisy. I didn't need any secret or phony friends. My assignment was tough enough and too time consuming to manage pretenders.

I didn't have the time or energy to watch for the daggers aimed at my back. Now, in retrospect, I don't believe all of these people were necessarily trying to destroy me or plotting my demise. I'd like to think it was not as nefarious as it seemed but rather their unpolished way of pushing me aside, given I was operating outside of the confines of the church's philosophy.

A lot of the brothers and some of the sisters believe women can serve and do other auxiliary things that assist the brotherhood but are not called to lead. There was no issue or problem with my teaching Sunday school to the children and young people. Furthermore, I was encouraged, supported and acknowledged in my fundraising efforts. I'll give them credit though; they sure did teach me how to raise money for the ministry. They taught me the importance and value of money. Even to this day, I love raising offerings for the people of God. However, I stepped way out of line when I touched the forbidden third rail of the Church of God in Christ: Women Pastors. And, I had the audacity to stand in the office of a pastor. "How dare Sybil think the Lord called her to pastor." "Who does she think she is?" The screams of displeasure rang out from peanut galleries and church pews across the state, regionally and even nationally.

"The Church of God in Christ does not have any women as pastors and we are not going to start now." Yeah, I guess in their eyes I had crossed that proverbial line in the sand and had gone too far. I guess you can say I took it to the point of no return. The stalwarts who professed to protect the "shield" were determined to silence and sit me down. Some leaders even thought they would make a name for themselves by managing me, offering their sound and wise counsel on what I should do. These wise men, and sometimes women, had all the answers except the one God gave me. The consensus amongst the leadership in both the local and national fellowship was that no woman belonged in the pulpit — never mind leading a church.

While some of the brother preachers were more discreet with their feelings than others, for the majority of them, I was an uncomfortable challenge to their theology and way of conducting ministry. Quite frankly, most of them wished I would just go away. There were cries of "If she really wants to be a pastor that bad, she can go and join a body that licenses women to be pastors. The episcopal faith will take her if she is really that adamant about the office. Shoot, she can even be a bishop with them."

Can you imagine the mindset of these people of God? But the toughest part for me during this season was that there were some members of my home church that were not comfortable with the controversial stance our ministry was taking. Some of them attempted to push forward to the front their favorite male minister hoping I would acquiesce and defer to them. They didn't want to be part of a church that was ostracized for having a female pastor. Even some of my members wanted to know why did Sybil have to disturb the status quo? Who was Sybil to challenge the leadership of the church and the great Bishop C. H. Mason's doctrinal structure? I had to look in the mirror and ask some tough questions myself. Who was I having *the Audacity to Lead?* I was on my second marriage; I needed to be taking care of my new husband. I was working a secular job and I had no pastoral training. By all accounts, I shouldn't have been fighting to lead a church. But that was the carnal man speaking and sometimes you have to rebuke your own thoughts and doubts and encourage yourself. So while the naysayers continued to beat the drum of why doesn't she just let one of the male elders lead the church I hunkered down and kept praying. Still they felt if I was just set on preaching, I could be an evangelist or an evangelist missionary. I could take appointments speaking for women's conferences and first ladies anniversaries. I could have been Mother Dunwoody or even State Supervisor. Wasn't that enough? No, it wasn't, because that's not what the Lord said. What was it that all these oracles couldn't understand? All these people that were so anointed and intelligent who were given over to prayer and study, yet they were unable to see the simplicity in an omnipotent God's choice.

Besides, I knew of other women who led churches and preached but didn't call themselves pastor and that was their choice and between them and their God, but the Lord didn't say that to me. He called me Pastor. The most ironic thing about this whole ordeal is that I really wasn't looking to be called pastor. It wasn't that important to me, the Lord assured me that I was called to do the job. However, I was aware that God had order and that we are supposed to give honor where honor is due and I had to be firm in my commitment and calling. But I understand the disrespect and lack of acknowledgement. My dad would often quote *Mark 6:4*: "*But*

Jesus said unto them, a prophet is not without honour, but in his own country, and among his own kin, and in his own house." Therefore, I figured it was par for the course. At the end of the day, all I wanted to do was fit in with the brethren and not be ridiculed, disrespected intentionally, hindered from completing my assignment. So for the sake of getting along and not ruffling feathers, for a season, I let the people call me the ridiculous title of "shepherdess." Shepherdess was less threatening, not biblical; but they didn't care, it made them feel superior to me and it kept them off my back. So I entertained their nonsense for a season until an overwhelming number of my members began to grow weary and angry with the disrespect and politics of the church. To my amazement, even some of my co-laborers began to express distaste in the title. One of the brother preachers, who is a mentee to me, came and spoke at the church one Sunday evening and admonished me and the members to get rid of what he referred to as a ridiculous title. I guess it was what some call confirmation and helped with my decision to lose the title. Dead and gone were the days of my being referred to as "Shepherdess." I had to stand and be what I was called to be, regardless of what the leaders and others thought about me.

With all love and deference, the church has some blatant hypocrisy that I believe is keeping us back and causing some to leave the fellowship. The leadership knew there were several women across the country running churches. They didn't sanction it but allowed it to go on for financial purposes. It was quite an ambiguous relationship, given they accepted the financial reports of churches headed by women but didn't recognize them. The church can't have it both ways and maintain full integrity. Politics in any organization can cause smart, ethical people to act in strange ways. However, given my assignment from the Lord I could not deter from the path. But to many of the folks, it was more about what was I trying to prove?

Then there was another faction of people I call conspiracy theorists whom had deeper, diabolical thoughts concerning my position as pastor. For example, a small and insignificant clique of troublemakers posed the theory that my father didn't say the Lord told him the mantle was falling to my leadership. Instead, they believed my assignment was a power move by the family to maintain control of the church. I can only imagine the nonsense that was said that I didn't hear.

Initially, I took that and all the rest of the foolish comments as personal attacks against me. Truthfully, some of the comments hurt me to the core. If you've never experienced agenda-driven, angry church people, then you can't fathom religious wrath. Being wounded in the House of the Lord often causes fatal wounds in your walk with Christ. You never expect to be injured in the House of the Lord because the church professes to be a spiritual hospital and safe haven from the world, so those wounds hurt more. Nonetheless, as Christians we have to have thick skin and be able to withstand the attacks of the enemy even when they occur in the House of the Lord. Subsequently, I thank God He didn't allow me to hear everything, because maybe I would have wavered in my conviction and doomed myself to damnation through disobedience.

Dealing with the leadership outside of the church was bad enough. But people, who I worshipped with for years, spent time at their homes and them at mine, had completely turned against me and began to take sides at the most vulnerable time of the ministry. And, instead of being on the Lord's side, they chose the side of the enemy. A number of times I was ready to turn my keys in and keep on moving. Countless times I said things to myself such as, "I don't need this" and "I'm out." But the Lord had a larger plan for the ministry and I had to lead it.

If I had kept focusing on what the people were saying, I would have given up; because really, it would have been so much easier to go sit in another church — maybe even a different organization. I would have been a great lay member. I could have attended Sunday school and church service, given my tithes and offering and then went home and enjoyed the rest of my week. I could have worn all my nice clothes and no one would have anything to say and I definitely would have had more money to spare. When the church needed a new boiler, furnace, windows, heating oil and many other things, I wouldn't be responsible and have to use my own money to make up the shortfall when the ministry fundraising didn't meet the financial obligations. When mother or sister needed help with rent, a light bill and food, I wouldn't have to decimate the church treasury and my personal savings to help meet the needs of the less fortunate in the church. It would have been a lot easier financially and in my personal life. In fact, I would have had a personal life. But God said, not so. He had other plans for me. He was molding me and requiring me to endure and serve in the capacity He outlined. I had to continue moving the church forward, which meant I had to endure disrespect and belittling, trying to serve the Lord. These slights and offenses not only occurred within the four walls of my church but also in district and state meetings.

Then some of those same brother preachers, who said I had no business preaching, would invite me to participate and speak at their fundraising and anniversary services. I would get up and say kind words, give liberally and help raise money for their offerings. Then these same fine gentlemen would have me ushered off to sit with the women. Meanwhile, the pastor and male elders sat in the pulpit. And to my dismay, they saw nothing wrong with their actions. In fact, it was completely normal and acceptable to them — talk about cognitive dissonance.

As a practice for many years, women were not allowed to preach from the pulpit in the Church of God in Christ. Today, they make some exceptions for the popular national evangelists and few others. But if you visit a church and it happens to be Women's Day, you will likely see the preacher, if she is female, preaching from the floor. To be completely honest, I felt a little disrespected and marginalized. But, I made the best of the archaic thinking, down on the floor preaching, in a large number of the churches I was invited to speak. I was able to look into the eyes and souls of the saints and meet them where they were and help empower them to live victorious lives through Christ. Still, I knew I was equal to the brothers in the eyes of God, so that was the only thing that truly mattered. Man might be but God is no respecter of persons. In any case, I was mature enough to know that the brothers' out-of-date beliefs didn't make them bad people or my adversaries but rather chauvinistic and unenlightened men whose thinking had yet to evolve. I stilled loved, prayed and supported the brothers. And, in most cases, I even returned and preached for them, helping to advance their visions and work.

Thus, in the final analysis, it wasn't important where I was preaching from, but rather who I was preaching for, which was my Lord and Savior and the people I was preaching to, His followers. I was there to serve the people and lift up the Kingdom. Although I was relegated to preaching from the floor, God elevated me. Therefore, it's important for me to let both men and women know, it's not about where man puts you but rather where God places you. *Psalm 75:6* makes it clear: *"For promotion comes neither from the east, nor from the west, nor from the south."* Real promotion comes from God.

I was thoroughly convinced that in the fullness of time, and hopefully before the Lord's triumphant return, God would do the work on them. In all actuality, they had two options, they would evolve or be left behind; not like left behind in the rapture sense, but rather left behind in the Kingdom becoming stale organizations not experiencing growth or producing fruit. God's church is a living, breathing organism that should become more enlightened over time. Let me be clear, I'm not referring to enlightenment in which we change our stance on holiness and the foundation of our beliefs, but rather we shift our thinking and positions on antiquated religious traditions and constraints that hinder progress.

Although it has been twenty-five years since I began my pastoral journey, a lot of the outlandish thinking remains. At times, I wonder about the psychological effects of the hierarchical tenets of the church. I totally believe in good leadership and I support effective leaders. However, good leaders must have vision; they must grow and evolve in their thinking and ways. Good leaders make others better around them. They challenge tradition and the status quo; they have the courage to throw out what's not working. They are fearless and unafraid to go against the consensus, even to their peril. Good leaders also know that there is a time and season for everything. But fundamentally, good leaders, or should I say effective leaders, must be teachable, reachable and touchable.

Three

It Doesn't Matter What They Think

"But I say unto you which hear, Love your enemies, do good to them which hate you." —Luke 6:27

While a small part of the leadership has evolved in their thinking, many of the old-school leaders still feel that only a man is qualified to successfully lead a ministry and has the right to preach. It's amazing how some of these deep biblical scholars could believe God spoke through a donkey but would not choose to use a woman. Unfortunately, this barbaric, prehistoric thinking has held many ministries back and kept some people from coming into their full potential.

In retrospect, I take no real offense at the chauvinistic mentality of the leadership or their outdated processes that hindered authentic spiritual growth. A lot of times, systems seem appropriate and beneficial at their inception, and in theory; however, once put into practice, they fail to accomplish the intended purpose.

Either way, I know God directed me through the process for my spiritual growth and development.

The Lord made me to prosper and flourish, and in turn, I learned to encourage, under duress and distress. I am ever grateful for the experience; it taught me not to be resentful with those who are out of touch and ignorant. I pray they come into a deeper understanding sooner than later. It's that anointing that makes the difference and it's the anointing that destroys the yokes. Whether I preach from the floor or the balcony, as long as I preach Christ and Him crucified, lives will be transformed.

However, I wish some of the brother preachers followed my lead and preached from the floor; they might have reached more of the lost, and maybe their churches would have more than a handful of members. Many of these self-proclaimed spiritual giants, those who are so amazing in their own eyes, seem to be missing the mark of inspiring men and women. Week in and week out, they preach to empty pews and chairs, decked out in three-piece suits and alligator shoes, pontificating, going through the rituals and routines, but no growth or transformation. I believe ministry is not a numbers game in relation to quantity of membership.

We are ministers of one and can be effective living a Christ-like life. Given that premise, some churches were designed to be small (but effective). Even today, mission churches have their place and mega ministries are not superior and not necessarily for everyone.

Conversely, at some point after you have been preaching 20 years, you have to determine if you are being effective and lives are being transformed, or is it more important that your ego be massaged, with the title of pastor. In the scriptures, we see that when the fig tree failed to produce, Jesus cursed the tree and it dried up and died. If ministries are not producing fruit, maybe it's time to start thinking about doing something else in the Kingdom besides the office of pastor. The souls of men and women are too important to be mishandled and or led by uninspiring, out-of-touch leaders who really should be sitting under a seasoned pastor.

I have two firm requirements before sending or nominating people to go forth in ministry. First, they must be thoroughly furnished with the Word of God. Being able to put a couple of scriptures together and hit a tune with the organ does not make you a preacher or a pastor. Just as any craftsman or professional person hones their craft, you must do the same: 2 Timothy 2:15 says: *"Study to show yourself approved unto God, a workman that needeth not to be ashamed, rightly dividing the word of truth."* Studying is a daily lifelong responsibility, not something that is done before you preach. I refuse to foist onto the world one more unqualified preacher who can't rightly divide the Word of God. Second, they must live a life that is consecrated and set apart for the Kingdom and be dedicated to serve. Only then do you begin to qualify for the position.

I attended and completed Bible school, going through a systematic study and teaching of the Bible. As a result, any and everybody I send forth into the world to minister will do the same. Consecration and a thorough knowledge of the word of God is a prerequisite.

Four

Your Gift Will Make Room For You

"Ye shall not need to fight in this battle. Set yourselves, stand ye still, and see the salvation of the Lord with you, O Judah and Jerusalem. Fear not, nor be dismayed. Tomorrow go out against them: for the Lord will be with you." —2 Chronicles 20:17

My ultimate goal in assuming the role of pastor was not an attempt to make some statement about women preachers, nor did I desire to compete with the brothers in ministry. Ministry is not a competition, nor is it a hobby. Ministry is a lifestyle. It's a seven-day-a-week vocation that requires impeccable integrity and commitment to people. It's a lifelong assignment that, on many occasions, can be thankless and overwhelming. The new role as pastor would prove to be my toughest assignment yet.

I was not into jockeying for the position because I really didn't want it. However, my desire was to please God and help transform the lives of His people. I figured since God chose me, He would equip me. I was quite sure He knew what He was doing. I didn't have anything to prove to man. Although I did want the brothers to know I was quite capable of doing the job. I simply wanted to do the work of the Lord with honor and integrity. In my father's passing, the Lord transformed my life and gave me the heart of a pastor. It was incumbent upon me to operate in that capacity. I needed to be the leader the Lord created and enjoy the opportunity for this journey. Deep down inside, I wanted to be a pastor like my father and reach people from all walks of life. I was going to emulate Jesus and represent His Kingdom with class, dignity and authenticity.

I wasn't standing and serving for recognition or acceptance. I was determined to stand and proclaim the good news of the gospel to 100 or 1,000 with fervor, honor and integrity. Ignorant Christians are precarious people. I use the term ignorant, as opposed to stupid, because I don't believe the people of God are stupid; however, some are quite ignorant. And thankfully for them, that can be remedied. Ignorance is defined as uninformed and unaware. The Apostle Paul in writing in the Book of Romans 10:1-2 addresses this very concern when he states: *"Brethren, my heart's desire and prayer to God for Israel is that they may be saved. For I bear them witness that they have a zeal for God, but not according to knowledge."* Ignorance can be caused by flawed doctrine or an exaggerated sense of self-importance or just plain stubbornness to the move of God. Whatever the cause, enlightenment can occur through the proper study of the Word of God. Nevertheless, there is still a faction of people who resist enlightenment and remain so caught up in who they think should lead a ministry. They remain clouded by their own haughtiness and ignorance. In the Apostle Paul's writing to Timothy, he describes them as: *"Having a form of godliness, but denying the power thereof: from such turn away."* —*2 Timothy: 3:5*. These self-aggrandizing people are dangerously out of touch with the Kingdom of God, to the point that you would think they are in possession of an invitation list to heaven, and they have the decision of whom God can use.

God called and used women for great works throughout the Bible, and I was confident in what the scripture stated in *Galatians 3:28: "There is neither Jew nor Greek, there is neither bond nor free, there is neither male nor female: for ye are all one in Christ Jesus."* I was and will always be 100 percent a lady — I like to look like a lady. I didn't then, nor do I now, believe that chivalry is dead. My thinking might be considered passé but I still think it's appropriate for a man to open the door for a lady, regardless of her stature or position. Call me old-fashioned but that's what I learned from my daddy. I am not a feminist preacher or anti-men. I love the brothers and respect them in their role and in the Kingdom of God.

For every person that comes into the Kingdom of God, there is an assignment. God has a specific job which only that particular person will do. God has endowed each of us with a sphere of influence, a group of people that look upon us for leadership and as examples. All people of God are ministers, even if only to our families, friends and especially non-believers with whom we have a relationship. Many of us may be the closest thing to a church or religious experience that some people will ever encounter or interact with. Therefore, it is truly incumbent upon us to live the life that we preach about.

With a large population of people turned off with the church experience, the world is looking for real people who profess salvation to stand in integrity and live what they preach. Shunning the very appearance of evil and wrongdoing must be a daily goal. We should strive to keep our hearts and minds under subjection and follow the instructions laid out for us in the Book of Romans, *"Present your bodies a living sacrifice holy and acceptable unto God."* —*Romans 12:1.* We are Christ's ambassadors to the world. The worst thing that could occur is for believers to be perceived as hypocrites or insincere people. The world is watching. Once you declare that you are living for God, you place your life under a microscope to be examined by all.

Unbelievers have an idea of what people of God should do, how they should look and how they should act. Our behavior is on trial and the last thing we want is a guilty verdict. Being convicted of impersonating a child of God is a major charge. How we act on our jobs, in the community and with our unsaved loved ones is important. There is no time for half-stepping and game playing.

In order to be the best we can be, God has to develop and discipline us in the way He sees fit. We don't have the authority to dictate what we will or will not go through. God is the Pilot of our lives and has navigated the perfect flight pattern, which if followed, will lead us from earth to heaven. Salvation is the only pre-requisite to begin effective service.

Although I grew up working and serving in the church, attended Bible school and was comprehensively trained in the Word of God, that collective group of accomplishments did not automatically make me a leader. God yet had to mold and guide me through His process. That's one of the main reasons we as believers say to our God, "Not our will but your will be done." God wants us to trust and believe that whatever He allows is for our good, for the preservation of our salvation and the surety of our spiritual growth.

God will remove all of the props out of our life and see if we will trust and serve Him as we testify. While going through the process, will we have the spirit of Peter and deny Him when the pressure becomes overwhelming? It's a lot easier to do a job for God when everything is going right in your life. When all of our bills are paid and we feel like we are up on top of the mountain, it's easy to shout with conviction and boldly testify to His goodness. God wants to see if we are willing to live our testimony and demonstrate that "keeping it real" aspect of our witness when we can't find favor. Can we still shout and encourage our brothers and sisters when we have no money, no job and no prospects? Can we talk about being "abundantly blessed" and "highly favored" when we are facing the grim reality of foreclosure and pending homelessness? What about when sickness is ravaging our bodies and the medical professionals have told us that it's terminal. Then whose report are we going to believe? Can we still talk about how good God is? What will be our testimony when we can't find the twins, grace and mercy? Until you have been there and spent the night, you have yet to be tested.

I have first-hand experience about that place which I call the "Dark Place." But within that dark place, I developed a "Dark Days Praise." Those are the days when things seem bleak and problems appear insurmountable, but you praise God anyway; much like the three Hebrew boys in the Old Testament, Meshach, Shadrach and Abednego, having the blessed assurance that even if God doesn't bring you out, you know He can.

Throughout the first twenty-five years of leadership as Pastor, God has removed every man-made support and crutch that I relied too heavily upon. The tough part was that He seemed to do it at the worst, possible times. It wasn't that I believed in anything more than I believed in God, but at times I placed too much faith in people and things. Let me be clear, we do need one another; God manifests Himself in our relationships. We need the fellowship and intimacy. However, we must be careful not to place too much faith in a person, while simultaneously realizing people are valuable and important. Consequently, seek to avoid putting unrealistic and impossible demands on people. It's a balancing act on a bumpy road. It was only because of a common theme in my life and a pivotal message, "Position Yourself," in my ministry that I was able to survive the bumps. Today, I call them bumps; however, at the time of their occurrence, they seemed like gigantic craters the size of the Grand Canyon, seeming nearly insurmountable.

One of my goals when counseling and witnessing to people, especially new converts, is to quickly tell them that God is the answer to all their problems. The scriptures let us know that: *"He will turn again, He will have compassion upon us; He will subdue our iniquities; and thou wilt cast all their sins into the depths of the sea."* —*Micah 7:19*. Notwithstanding, we must possess the faith to tackle the problems and have the blessed assurance that God will see us through. Additionally, I am quick to inform them that once you accept Christ in your life not all problems end. For some the real challenges begin, because once you have God in your life, the enemy seeks to destroy you and your relationship with God. Accepting Christ is not some magic pill to cure all your problems, but rather a start of the best relationship you will ever have in your life. Yes, God throws our past transgressions into the sea of forgetfulness; however, God has some eternal laws that must be honored. In the Book of Galatians, the scripture tells us: *"Do not be deceived: God cannot be mocked. A man reaps what he sows." —Galatians 6:7.* He is a Sovereign God who directs and guides our paths and gives us salvation.

We are more carefree and complacent, as opposed to the saints just a generation ago. We feel we can master time and even His return. You can blame it on the new age or technology or what have you. Today, people have a cavalier attitude about service and dedication to God. Our existential disposition leads us to think we can master even God's behavior as we live for the moment and throw caution to the wind in regards to eternal consequences. Our level of arrogance is only championed by our need to be seen and heard. As the new-age Christian, we think we have arrived and have such a deeper understanding of the Spirit and move of God. When in reality, we are not nearly as spiritual as many of the old-time saints, with all of our education and training, the numerous conferences we conduct and attend, and the general information overload. We are no further along than the saints a generation ago. With all of our new fancy praise songs, our worship teams and five-piece orchestras, we may entertain — but the lives of the people are not being transformed.

My mind and spirit hearken back to a time when some old mother would simply stand up and sing one of the old call-and-response songs like "Power;" and by the time we got finished singing we were in the presence of the Lord. Then the preacher would deliver "What Thus Saith the Lord." No, they were not versed in the Greek and Hebrew translations of the scriptures; and no, the preachers didn't properly exegesis the text all the time, but they studied till God gave them a word for His people. Unlike today, where so many preachers pick a topic to talk about and find scriptures to back up their thesis, feeding us a steady diet of "What Say Them?" as opposed to "What Thus Saith the Lord." Additionally, they had incomparable integrity and believed in lifting up a standard for the Lord. Those preachers in my young days were quick to tell you that you had to be holy. They were preachers who stood firm on the command, *"Because it is written, Be ye holy; for I am holy."* —*1 Peter 1:16*. And if I did a comparison of the saints then and now, I don't think we would measure up so well against them. In fact, I believe we would be found substandard and wanting.

Conversely, more and more I understand *Matthew 24:22* when the Lord says: *"And except those days should be shortened, there should no flesh be saved: but for the elect's sake those days shall be shortened."* With all the depravity and despair going on in the world, the Lord is soon to return. And that's a phrase that has been tossed around for hundreds of years, yet is truer today than it has ever been. The signs are all around; still countless people seem oblivious to the obvious.

I can remember in my teenage years the saints constantly stating, "Look for the Lord to return." We thought that was their way of attempting to scare us into living holy. They would tell us to look for God because He was coming real soon. They would say: "If He doesn't come in the morning, look for Him in the afternoon; if He doesn't come in the afternoon, look for Him in the evening." They waited for His triumphant return with baited-breath. It got so bad to the point that I was so scared and some nights I didn't want to go to sleep, for fear of missing the Lord when He came. The last thing we wanted was to be left behind for the Tribulation. Our desire was to go with Him on the first trip. In retrospect, I'm thankful for those old saints putting expectancy and urgency in our walk with Christ; that same urgency and expectancy so many seem to lack today. However, I try to instill some of that resolution in my members, frequently making mention of God's warning to us about our lackadaisical ways, compelling the members, as the prophet Amos did when he stated: *"Woe to them that are at ease in Zion and trust in the mountain of Samaria, which are named chief of the nations, to whom the house of Israel came!"* —*Amos 6:1*

Five

Preparation For The Journey

"Before I formed you in the womb I knew you, before you were born I set you apart: I appointed you as a prophet to the nations."
—Jeremiah 1:5

Over the course of my life, I have developed a complete dependency on Jesus for which I am not ashamed. As far back as I can recall, when I developed a real understanding of God and His will, I have been in the most wonderful, loving and blessed relationship with Him. We have a love affair that seems to get stronger each day. My passion and enthusiasm brings me to profess my true confession that I can't live without Him. We have been together so long that I tremble to imagine what my life would be without Jesus. One thing I am absolutely sure of is that I have no desire to ever find out. It was the psalmist King David who said, *"As the deer panteth after the waterbrook, so doeth my soul after thee O God."* —*Psalm 42:1*

The Lord saved, sanctified and filled me with the precious Holy Ghost as a teenager. Sadly, that is something that seems to be passé now. With the risk of sounding old-fashioned, back when I was a teenager, receiving the baptism of the Holy Ghost was something we were proud of and cherished. And although it was a gift, we worked for it. We tarried on the altar all night praying to be filled. Those saved, sanctified, old mothers worked with us making sure we had it for real. I'll tell you this much, if you came up speaking in tongues and it was not of the Spirit of God, they would let you know. They would say: "Oh no baby, that ain't it. Get back down there and keep tarrying." They were so powerful that if you caught a foul spirit they would cast it out of you without missing a beat. With authority under the Holy Ghost they would yell, "Come out demon." They didn't care if you were embarrassed nor did they care about your feelings. Your feelings were an afterthought, but your soul was a priority.

The things that go on in the House of the Lord, and are accepted by man, are not necessarily of God. But today's Christian is markedly different from those just a generation ago. Yes, some things were silly. For example, women were not going to hell for wearing pants or if their skirts came above their knees. No, "red lipstick" was not going to make the woman's lips fall off or prevent them from seeing Jesus. However, some of that structure that was put in place kept a portion of the young women and men from straying and falling into temptations. It kept a lot of people saved. While some still got caught up in negative behavior, a lot of that structure was clearly beneficial. Actually, I wish we had some of those saved, sanctified, old mothers serving with us today, willing to work with the new converts; maybe our churches would have more power.

We live in the time when new converts go to the altar, give the preacher their hands and God our hearts, then feel they are saved and ready to preach the next month. I'm only half joking about them preaching next month. Those old Pentecostal preachers and mothers didn't allow such things. They would sit you down and tell you: "Son, daughter you are not ready yet, sit and wait on your calling." While not all of their rebuke and admonishment was scripturally based, their hearts were in the right place. Now we have become so educated and enlightened we forget the bridges that brought us over and minimize the effects that they had on us.

Conversely, in this instant gratification society, salvation and the route to salvation seem to have been shortened. I make it clear in my teachings there are no shortcuts in the Kingdom of God. You must do the work, make the sacrifices and by faith trust in the Lord. On the other hand, that's not saying it takes forever to accept Christ, but this drive-through salvation nowadays has led to wishy-washy church people who seem to be moved by every whim, doctrine and hurt feelings. As a result, we have a large group of people who are finding it more difficult to hunker down and get rooted in a Bible-believing church and learn God's Word, because the moment they hear something they don't like or face rebuke, they are out the door and off to the next church or worse, their couch to watch their favorite television pastor. There is no accountability in the television pastor and no expectation for the believer. Serving the Lord is not easy nor is it comfortable.

I have been serving the Lord for a long time and like the songwriter says, "I am in no ways tired." Furthermore, I am fully determined to go all the way with Jesus. Sometimes when I get a little weary and tired I can hear my dad saying: "Sybil, true saints of God don't rust out, we wear out." My heart reminisces back to those delightful family dinners at the old Valley's Steakhouse when my dad would teach us about the Kingdom of God. He created that phrase because he believed that it was our responsibility as servants of the Most High God to never stop working until God calls us home. It was most appropriate because there is always something to do in the Kingdom of God. As a result, whenever I take in new members, I let them know they have a short grace period to get to know the other members and make themselves knowledgeable of the church practices and statement of beliefs. Then they must find something to do in the House of the Lord because we don't have bench members. God has a job for each of us. My job is to preach and lead, but they must figure out what job the Lord has for them or I will assign them one. Time is of the essence. Life is short and there is a dying world that needs a Savior. *"I must work the works of Him that sent me, while it is day: the night cometh, when no man can work."* —John 9:4

Sometimes I sit in amazement reflecting on the amount of time I have been in ministry, fifty-plus years, seems like almost yesterday. One Friday night, November 1959, during one of our annual church revivals, I had my transformation moment. Nowadays they say that "Aha Moment," whatever you want to call it; it's that moment which changed my life. My father had invited a guest evangelist from out of town to come and minister the Word of God. My father knew a lot of people from all over the country. He was a very loving and friendly man, so people loved to fellowship with us and many pastors trusted him. Because of that trust, they would allow and, in many cases, send their elders to us to preach. Consequently, it's important to note that God sends people to you, and they may not be the people you expect or the people you are looking for.

The word God has for you sometimes may not be from your pastor or some popular prophet or evangelist. It could come from a child in Sunday school; it could come from an old church mother singing off-key banging on a beat-up tambourine or a song the choir sings during worship service. That tailored word could even come from the benediction, while you are putting on your coat, getting ready to walk to your car. Now let me clarify before I go any further, that the pastor is the angel of the house in which you worship. In addition, the pastor is the one who prays and watches over your soul. Have your pastor confirm and decipher the word you receive. The reason being, there are many false teachers, preachers and prophets who prey on weak and new babes in Christ. My dad protected us from those who were not appropriate. He was our spiritual guardian and true under-shepherd. A lot of the preachers were just getting their start, and for all intents and purposes, were really practicing on us. But thanks be to God that there are no coincidences and truly as His Word says: *"And we know that all things work together for good for those who love God, who are called according to his purpose."* —*Romans 8:28*. In the Kingdom of God, nothing just happens; God always has a purpose and a plan.

But this particular guest evangelist he had speaking for the service, was seasoned and well versed in the scriptures. She regularly traveled across the country and preached at many different churches. I distinctly remember she was a powerful preaching woman, small in stature, big in anointing and bigger in God. She spoke clearly and practical delivering, "Thus Saith the Lord." She didn't have a catchy title to her message nor did she tell you to tap or high five your neighbor every five minutes like so many of the preachers do today. The evangelist was not the most charismatic or eloquent speaker; nevertheless, she spoke powerful words from the Bible, and I could feel her authenticity resound through the speakers shaking the walls. On that night the evangelist simply preached the unadulterated Word of God. She had the key — God on the inside. The message was transforming. Her message to the church was simple, basic and appropriate and her focus was on true holiness. She did her best to convince our congregation that in life and service to God there were two distinct choices, "Holiness or Hell." And to this day, our journey in salvation boils down to that choice. It's that black and white, and there was no in-between or temporary holding spot. We were taught, and I still believe, if you die in sin, in hell will you lift up your eyes.

As she began to talk about how we live our lives and the fact that we must live holy and our failure to do so would result in dire consequences, the realness of what she was speaking began to resonate and manifest in my spirit. She began to speak about the eternal pain and torment of hell. Her vivid descriptions shook me to the core. I trembled at the thought of living in eternal torment and damnation. Yes, there is something after this life and please don't ever allow yourself to be lulled into a state of ease. A fear came over me like I had never experienced in my life. After hearing that life-changing message, I knew I had to live holy. At that moment, I decided to give my life to God for real and with all sincerity. After she delivered her powerful message, the evangelist beckoned all who desired prayer to meet her at the altar. I was so compelled to move that I jumped in the line. As I approached her to pray for me, I felt an incredible, overwhelming feeling that I had never before experienced in my life, which I later realized was that of the Holy Ghost. That night I was baptized and filled with the Holy Ghost and my life was transformed. I was a new creature.

Some people are unaware and have misinformation about the Holy Ghost. There are misnomers and untruths about the Holy Spirit. However, God himself said that it is for us, our children and our children's children. Jesus, upon His ascension, let us know that He would not leave us comfortless and that He would send us a Comforter, that being the Holy Ghost. My dad stressed the importance of the Holy Ghost. He told me I could only stay saved for so long without the baptism of the Holy Ghost. So much of what was practiced a decade ago would be shunned in today's church. Political correctness has crept into the church and it has not helped to improve the work.

As a young girl, my family and I frequently attended church. And when I say attended church, I mean every time the doors opened for service we were there, ready to experience a wonderful move of the Lord. Church was not just a part of our lives; it was our very life. We arrived on time and didn't leave until the service ended, and that could be midnight or later. Then on special occasions and during certain periods of the year we held revivals and shut-ins (where we stayed in the church for days at a time); something hardly any churches do now. Sometimes we were closed up in the church for several days at a time with the purpose of spiritual deliverance, answers and breakthroughs. We believed in sacrificing for God and trusting Him to do great and important things in our lives. We firmly believed that our destiny and success was tied to God. We felt every sacrifice we made for God was honored and our sacrifices were for His glory. Nowadays it doesn't seem as though people desire to make real sacrifices for God.

A lot of talking and lip service is what you hear. I was taught as a young girl that actions speak louder than words. Unfortunately, many people today don't pray with fervor until their backs are against the wall. Times have definitely changed. I often think with so many of the saints who have medical conditions in their bodies and rely on medication to stay well, could they or would they be able to participate in shut-ins and weeklong fasts? Sadly because of the times we live in and the litigious disposition of society, we probably would have to have the members sign waivers of releases of prosecution, ensuring that the church would not be liable in the event of someone's sickness. I would hate to be the church that falls into the hands of a defense attorney that takes that case. Back then we knew that everything we needed was tied up in God. In such a short period of time, things have drastically changed and not all for the better. A lot of people today, more specifically, people working in ministry say, *"It didn't or doesn't take all of that"* referring to the old way, but I am not so sure that's an accurate assumption. Given the condition of the body of Christ and the people who profess salvation, I think the jury is still out.

Salvation has never been about our attire. Clothes don't make the saints, the Spirit of God makes us. Our true desire is to be clothed in His righteousness. Nevertheless, there is still an appropriate way that you come before a holy God. I am not going to fall prey or allow the people I have leadership over to be hoodwinked into thinking that anything goes. I don't believe in giving a blanket license to the "come as you are group," who sometimes appear to be usurping power by encouraging believers to wear anything they want to church. This superficial secular leaning faction of the church attempts to water down the worship service and push the provocative envelope to the edge. If we are not wise and careful, the "clothes issues" can be a tool of the enemy to distract and discourage new converts; or worse, set up power dynamics that divert concentration away from the central theme which is Christ and Him crucified. As a result, we end up bogged down about a Trojan horse issue of clothes, while causing us to miss the essence of service.

Our true enemy and adversary want us to bite and devour one another. The enemy would love to see us waste time fighting about clothing and other superficial issues. We believed in wearing our best before God, but that doesn't mean you can't wear jogging pants to church. You are not going to hell for that. Nevertheless, if you have "dressy clothes," why not wear them? Present the best you to God. Some are quick to quote, not only inaccurately, but out of context, the scripture referring to come as you are. It's primarily referring to you, the person. Throughout the Bible, scriptures urge us to come to God as we are. Meaning whatever condition you are in, come to God, with your baggage, your faults and shortcomings; whatever state you find yourself in — come. So by all means make your way to a Bible-believing church; the fellowship will do you well.

Six

My Role Model

"Before I formed thee in the belly I knew thee; and before thou camest forth out of the womb I sanctified thee, and I ordained thee a prophet unto the nations." —Jeremiah 1:5

Being a leader in ministry is something predetermined by God. You don't just wake up one day and decide that you are going to be a pastor and open a church if you have not been called by God. Unlike any other profession, such as law or medicine where you complete a systematic study and meet the proper requirements and are awarded a license or become eligible to practice, ministry work is completely different.

However, when God has a calling on your life, His will is done at His appointed time. Regardless of your status in life, personal preparations, goals and ambitions, God's plan prevails. The Lord God had a plan for my life and prepared it before the foundation of the world. The evangelist He dispatched to our church the night I accepted Christ and received the Holy Ghost, at age 16, was not happenstance, but part of His plan. My dad's teaching and impartation was for God's specific purpose and plan. Everything I encountered on my journey was orchestrated by the hand of God. The poor decisions and bad choices I made were covered by His grace.

Before becoming a pastor, my dad started his ministry work as a deacon. He worked tirelessly for the church and his pastor. After an incredible commitment and dedication to his leader, the Lord called him to start a church. He jumped in with both feet. My father followed God in every step of this journey and did not make a move until he was sure that it was under the direction of the Lord, even down to the name of the church. He would often tell the story of how God came to him in a dream and gave him the name of the church, "Little Zion Church of God in Christ." His example of faith was a major part of my ability to accept the challenge to lead. He had been my rock support from day one. I was the apple of his eye, and he meant the world to me.

If an alien had ever come down to this planet and wanted to know what a true father was, I would have introduced him to my dad. He placed me on a pedestal, but yet always made me honor and serve God. When I had taken some time away from the church and ministry, my dad preached to me and encouraged me to seek the Lord. He told me that I had to act as though I was still serving God whenever I was in his presence. He said, "If you ain't saved, you better act like you are when you are around me."

Dad or "Grampy," as we affectionately called him was a loving man. He had what seemed to be unlimited compassion for the people of God. Till this day, I am still amazed at how much he cared for the saints. There were numerous times throughout my youth when saints who lived in other states would travel into town. My father would insist that they stay at our house. That was only the beginning. My Mom would have to prepare food for them, and we would have to give up our beds. I remember getting out of my warm, comfortable bed at two in the morning, having to go sleep on the living room floor space. At the time I didn't understand or necessarily agree with his decisions, especially when they involved my getting out of bed at 2:00 a.m.; but as time passed, I understood. The saints use to sing a song: "Further along we will know more about it, Further along we will understand why." Dad was sowing seeds of faith and love that I would harvest later in life. He was a powerful religious leader in our community. These days people judge a man's effectiveness on superficial things: Is he or she on television? Does he or she speak at the newest and biggest conferences? Is he or she part of the elite preaching circle? We believe the true measure of an individual is his or her integrity and commitment to the Lord and their family. Do they live what they preach? Do they love their brother and do they work to advance the Kingdom of God? These are the questions that have to be answered in the affirmative to make a real impact. Jesus said, "You will know them by their fruit." —*Matthew 7:16*. My dad did all of those things, but even more than that, he was a great father to me and my siblings. In addition, he was a spiritual father to the children in our ministry and a host of young preachers trying to find their way.

He was authentic in his service to the Lord but was not so holy and righteous that he refused to associate with the people who had yet to come into the full knowledge of God, nor was he shortsighted in teaching us things about the world. He would say we live in the world, but we are not of the world; this was a clear distinction with honor. Some leaders and pastors rob the people they serve of living a complete life.

My dad knew there was more to life than just church, and that didn't make him any less holy, sanctified or committed to the Kingdom of God. He was unconventional, unorthodox and light years ahead of his time. He did things that some Christians and religious leaders might sit and judge back in his day. He wanted me to have a full well-rounded life. For example, on a couple of occasions, my dad took me to the local dog track. At the dog track, you would see all kinds of people. Ninety-nine percent of them had no religion and only called on God to win the $2 quinella (a type of wager) or thank God when their bets won or placed. With the number of saints that attend the gambling casinos today, I am sure many of you know what I am talking about. While we didn't place any wagers, it was still quite exciting and without risk. As we watched the dogs run around the track, he taught me a valuable lesson on life and the world. He explained how "Swifty the Rabbit." was a type of sin. He said no matter how fast those dogs run they will never catch up to Swifty. Then he made the connection for us in our daily walk. He explained in life sin will cause us to chase after things we will never and should never get and will lead us off the course.

My dad was a spiritual giant but a great daddy as well. He loved to read the funny papers or the comic section as we refer to them now. He loved to laugh. I don't think he knew that laughter produced endorphins, but he knew that laughter was good for the soul. He was a hard-working man, with a full-time job while also serving full-time as the pastor of our church. In spite of all that, he found time to take me to special places. One of our favorite annual events was our trips to Rockefeller Center, ice skating at Christmas, followed by shopping at Macy's in New York City. It was very important to him that I experience life outside of the four walls of the church, and it wasn't a sin to have fun.

I am not going to rewrite or create revisionist history. My dad was far from perfect. He was flawed and dare I say that his feet slipped. He made mistakes, but he always kept a repenting heart and never tried to cover his own sin. When he did go too far, he owned up to his deeds and took his punishment like a man. He showed equity with all. I'm grateful for all the invaluable lessons he gave me. His example and teaching taught me to love the people I serve for who they are and what the Lord called them to be; then teach them, nurture them and mentor them, but also rebuke and reprove all with loving-kindness.

Seven

A Hard Lesson Learned

"But the Lord stood at my side and gave me strength, so that through me the message might be fully proclaimed and all the Gentiles might hear it. And I was delivered from the lion's mouth."
—2 Timothy 4:17

Church or religious people, as opposed to "Kingdom Members," especially those who have yet to be truly delivered from a life of sin, can be quite dangerous. These new-age hypocrites know how to quote scriptures, especially when it comes to someone whom they want to put in their proverbial place or tell-off someone they may not agree with. They know the church protocol and when to sit, stand and clap. They have memorized a handful of scriptures and now they are spiritually deep — yet they have no power.

The Bible is not a bludgeon used for the purpose of attacking people with whom you disagree or feel superior. Rather the Holy Bible is a sacred writ to be reverenced. It is a tool for inward reflection and transformation, filled with God's instruction for eternal life. When used for its intended purpose, it results in great victory for the readers and doers of its instructions. When we devote time to improving ourselves, as opposed to judging others, we will be more empowered. The Book of Matthew 7:3 asks the question: *"Why do you see the speck in your brother's eye but fail to notice the beam in your own eye?"* Our focus should be directed on the person we see when we look in the mirror.

Using the Bible to manipulate and control people is at best, bad taste and at worst, a sin. When people use the Word of God to verbally beat up a person, especially one who is hurting or may have been overtaken in a sin or transgression, they become the hypocrites. God's Word is a weapon and is referred to as a two-edge sword that cuts so finely it can separate bone from marrow. However, we, the believers, use the Word to fight the enemy — not our brothers and sisters. We use the Word to uplift the faithful and those yet to be converted. In addition, we use it to rebuke and reprove. We are not supposed to use the Word of God to prove people wrong or for the purposes of humiliation. We are to tell the truth and we do so with love and kindness. The prophet Jeremiah stated: *"The Lord hath appeared of old unto me, saying, Yea, I have loved thee with an*

everlasting love: therefore with loving-kindness have I drawn thee."
—Jeremiah 31:3

Angry and spiteful church people do more harm than good especially when it comes to advancing the Kingdom of God. The last thing a non-believer wants to see is a churchgoer shouting around the church, proclaiming victory one minute and then condescending the next: looking down on others who have been overtaken in sin. We, as saints, have been called to uplift and edify. And believers should be mindful when using the Word to exact out anger or dominance over a fellow saint, you also will be judged.

When I got ready to get married, my dad gave me away with honor. He let me know that even though I was leaving his house and cleaving to my husband, he would always be there for me as my pastor and my dad. He believed my marriage was not going to last; however, he had to let me go through the process. He was prophetic in many ways and his life experiences made him able to see trouble and bad situations before they developed. Six months after leaving my dad's house, I knew I had made a big mistake, but I was determined to make it work. However, I could not fathom how something that felt so right in the beginning turn out to be so dreadfully wrong?

I wasn't perfect, but boy was I spoiled. Maybe I set my standards and expectations too high, but that was partly my dad's fault because he was my living example of what a husband should be. So how in the world did I get caught up in this web of maltreatment, and more importantly, why? What was the lesson I was supposed to learn through all this heartache and pain? I guess in order for me to be able to minister to women about overcoming, I had to endure pain and disappointment. My real life testimony would be an example to many, providing the courage to make hard choices. But that assumption didn't help me with the misinformed church people. After my marriage ended, I can remember some of the church people, the ones with real zeal but lacking knowledge saying, "Don't you know God hates divorce." Yes, I know in the Book of Malachi the Lord spoke about His displeasure of divorce in the context of Israel's particular period of time. Conversely, I'm also aware that according to the Bible, marriage is a lifetime commitment. However, God also gives authorization for divorce in specific circumstances. I don't believe the Lord desired for me to be beaten and abused.

Furthermore, I already felt terrible about my situation. The last thing I needed was uninvited criticism, especially when it was in error. It was hard enough to muster up every ounce of faith and courage within me to move forward. I was terrified about what was ahead as I entered into a new phase of my life. Having literally gone through hell over the previous few years and done everything conceivably possible to provide my children with some semblance of normalcy, I had to let my sons know that it was not normal or appropriate for a man to hit a woman.

After enduring such dreadful heartache and pain, I had to choose life and the health and well-being of my children over pretense. What others thought about my life's decision wasn't important to me. I was the one living in complete turmoil and chaos which had become extremely violent and life threatening. It didn't matter what the talkers thought about my situation or even me. They didn't have to live with this sick man. Given the situation had become unbearable, I had to make a move. The final straw was the night my middle son, Andre, who was about four at the time, witnessed his father in a fit of rage strike me. That amazing brave boy stood up to defend me and told his father, "If you ever touch my mom again, I will hurt you." Although I was in such emotional pain, my heart went out to this boy who displayed the courage of a lion, willing to do whatever was necessary to protect me. I knew at this point things had gotten completely out of control and I had to get out for the sake of my children. The next day we left; literally with the clothes on our backs. I didn't know what the future held, but I had to pick up the pieces and move on. If I didn't make a move, the future with him was surely death. So for this sister to stand in front of me arrogantly, clothed in hypocrisy, telling me about how the Lord hates divorce was a little too much for me to handle. The last thing I needed was this sister's self-righteous judgement, quoting the precious Word of the Lord out of context. Thank God, I was able to hold my peace, but in my mind I wanted to say don't you know God hates fornicators, adulterers and liars too. A liar doesn't even have the ability to plead his case in the sight of God. Nevertheless, the Spirit of God allowed me to keep my tongue in check. Additionally, my position in the church and my commitment to the pastor wouldn't allow me to act in an inappropriate manner. But boy I'll tell you it sure felt good for a minute to at least think about telling her off in my mind.

My father would always say, "Once you speak it out of your mouth, you can't take it back and it is forever out in the universe." So I knew I couldn't stoop down to her level and besides I never wanted to intentionally hurt or wound anyone — even my haters and enemies. My dad told me a familiar story when I was a kid that said, "Sticks and stones may break my bones, but names will never hurt me." I think as I have matured and worked in ministry, I realized that although I know he meant it with good intentions, words actually do hurt. In fact, hurtful words are so damaging they can kill the spirit, destroy the religious experience and cause some to turn away from God. Since we are Christ's ambassadors and His representatives on earth, we must be careful of the words we use. Our words and actions should not be the cause of people, more specifically non-believers, being turned off by the church and the Kingdom experience. The Prophet Jeremiah spoke concerning the use of our words. He said, *"They make ready their tongue like a bow, to shoot lies…"* —Jeremiah 9:3. We, as Christians, are not treacherous people. One eye-opening lesson I learned is that just because people go to church every Sunday, that fact alone does not qualify them to be a saint of God. More and more I'm finding out that some of these same people I thought were so sainted were not as pure as the driven snow that they professed. They had stuff in their closets, which if exposed, would have been disastrous. Some people attend church for covert reasons, and their hearts and minds have yet to be transformed and changed. As a result, there will always be a small group of people who use church as an escape mechanism. These people go to church to get rid of their problems for a few hours and escape the real life issues that consume them. They are resistant to commit and change but comfortable in finding a scapegoat or temporary relief. Others go looking for something, and unfortunately, the something they are looking for is not necessarily Jesus, but rather a handout, husband or a hook-up. Some have ulterior motives and hidden agendas and the church is simply a means to an end. Actions and motives speak louder than vain oblations and fake sincerity. Lukewarm saints are the worse. They do more damage than the hell raisers do. That's why in the Book of Revelations 3:16, God says: *"So then because thou art lukewarm, and neither cold nor hot, I will spew thee out of my mouth."* God hates those "church people — hypocrites" that possess the spirit of the church of Laodicea.

Humility and learning to remain silent builds strength. So I accepted the "I told you so" and the "you should have known better." Deep down inside, at times it hurt me, but we live by the consequences of the decisions and choices we make.

Had I stayed in that terrible relationship, those same people would have been talking about how stupid I was to stay with a man who abuses and embarrasses me. However, my safety, security and peace of mind far outweighed the pretense and the "chitter chatter" some foolish people would spew.

Eight

When You Think The Unthinkable

But he said to me: "My grace is sufficient for you, for my power is made perfect in weakness. Therefore I will boast all the more gladly of my weaknesses, so that the power of Christ may rest upon me." —2 Corinthians 12:9

Although my marriage ended horrendously, one good thing which resulted from it was that God blessed me with three of the greatest sons a mother could ever want, each special in his own way. Each of my sons is an independent thinker who believes in me and supports me in different ways. We don't always agree, but that's what makes our relationships healthy and special.

The marriage didn't work. There was no mistake — only blessings and lessons. However, my advice to everyone is to listen to your parents and elders when it comes to marriage and picking a mate, especially the ones who have successful marriages. I know love is blind and most times in life you can't pick those with whom you fall in love. But parents, I mean ones who have a sure foundation in the Word of God, know trouble when they see it. My parents could spot a loser from a mile away. They cautioned me about my ex-husband and told me what I was getting into, but I still chose to go through it. I was a big girl and I learned a big lesson. My first marriage caused me many sad days and many sleepless nights. Yet, after a long period of time, my ex-husband and I were able to set aside our differences and remain cordial. Christ can cure all things. He can help you bind bitterness. Also, He can help you see the best in all people. God will replace a stony and broken heart with one of flesh.

As I began to increase my participation in ministry and working in the capacity that God called me, it seemed as though I was gaining strength and courage. However, deep on the inside at my core, I was still hurting emotionally. Actually, I was a complete wreck. You see to be completely honest, early on I knew my marriage was in trouble, but I tried everything short of balancing on my head to make it work. I would have done that if I thought it could have saved my marriage. No one really knew the severity of my pain. There were things I shared with some confidants, but even still I couldn't share it all. One, it was too embarrassing, and two, I was fearful of being judged. My struggle was a continuous fight. I was my own worst enemy — it was a battle within. The only person I could cry out to and be completely forthright about everything concerning the marriage was Jesus. So I had to cry on His shoulder every night when the children went to bed. My heart had been badly bruised and my spirit was nearly crushed. I nearly lost my mind. Today, they would have probably diagnosed me as clinically depressed and had me on all kinds of medications. Those old mothers would tell me: "Daughter, weeping only endures for a night and joy comes in the morning." They would frequently quote from the Book of Isaiah 26:3: *"God will keep you in perfect peace, if you keep your mind stayed on Jesus."* Yeah, I knew this but tell me what to do when I can't keep my mind stayed on Him. What do I do when my problems seem bigger than I can handle? What do I do when I can't keep the faith? I'm broken, and I don't need church people telling me to hold on, but rather lifting me up and helping me hold on. I needed them to hold my arms up like Aaron and Hur held up the arms of Moses when he was weak and tired.

The feelings of failures, despair and emptiness seemed to constantly consume me. The enemy discouraged me at every turn and I couldn't get any peace. I served the Prince of Peace, yet had no peace within. Finally, I got to the point where I felt like I couldn't endure the torture any longer. I wanted the pain to end and if that meant death, then so be it. Early one Friday morning I had decided to do what was once the inconceivable, and that was to end my life. The enemy has cunning ways, distorting reality, causing you to believe things will never get better, and as a result, you are better off dead. In fact, the serpent romanticizes the thought of suicide and attempts to make it conceivable and, in some instances, right-minded in your eyes. As a church girl all my life, we were always told that there were two things we could never do: bear false witness on the Holy Ghost and commit suicide. The saints of old told us God can't forgive you for these things. They would let us know that there is no repentance from the grave.

Just a few short years ago, my life was prospering. I was on top of the world. I was happy, and had a bright future ahead of me. I had everything to live for. Now, I was preparing for my departure from this world. After all the teaching I received, the enemy was able to convince me that ending my life was the only option. I knew that God hated for us to destroy what He created, but the pain was so bad that I was selfishly ignoring the known. After all the preaching, teaching and prayers that had been prayed over me, I was yet willing to end my life. People of God, it's important to know that as flesh, we can be put in situations that make us weak, causing us to succumb to the enemy. But don't beat yourself up, sometimes we lose fleshly battles. Our Savior lets us know that the spirit is willing and the flesh is weak.

God knew how bad I was suffering inside and He knew my heart. And He promised to never leave me or forsake me. Nevertheless, in my head, I went over and over different scenarios to end my life. Finally, I arrived at the one I thought would be the easiest and least painful. The best place to do it was Carson Beach in South Boston. I would go there and end all my suffering and hurt, and the storm of life would be over. That evening I drove my car to Carson Beach. It was the perfect location. The beach was closed for the season and there was no one around for miles. There would be no one to witness or try and talk me out of my decision. I arrived nervous, but determined. My entire life flashed before me as I sat there with the car idling. I began to talk to myself to work up the nerve to hit the gas pedal and never look back. All I had to do was drive the car off the embankment and it would be over. While on the embankment, I sat in the car trying to muster up the nerve to hit the accelerator and end it all. Okay, I decided now was the time. As I lifted my foot and slammed it down on the accelerator, suddenly out of nowhere a Boston policeman appeared, approaching my car. The officer startled me to the point that I almost had a heart attack. "Where did he come from?" I was completely alone out here. "What is going on?"

The officer came closer to my vehicle and motioned for me to roll down the window. I was completely flustered. I followed his order and lowered my window. He was an older Caucasian with a thick Irish accent. He asked me: "Ma'am what are you doing out here this time of night?" I didn't quite know what to say. I was still baffled about where he came from. If I told this man the truth, I could end up in jail, or worse, locked in some psych ward at Boston State Hospital. But for some reason, sometime later, I realized it was the Spirit of God which led me to tell him the truth. I told him I wanted to die. I shared with him how the cares of this world had overwhelmed me so much that I had decided to take my life. I broke down and just started weeping uncontrollably. Amazingly, he began to comfort and encourage me. We talked about my family life situations, my sons and the issues that led me to Carson Beach to end it all. I was able to open up to him in a manner that I couldn't with any of my church family and friends. Something about this man was different. He told me how I had so much to live for. His kind and supportive words brought me such a sense of comfort. Then I began to think what would have happened had I gone through with my plan. I would have left my three sons back here motherless. I felt horrible about wanting to do such a selfish act. Because my life had become so out of control and unmanageable, I was ready to hurt more people. My mom and dad would have been crushed by my actions; worse, I would have spent eternity in hell. What in the world was I thinking? Were things really as bad as I thought they were? Thank you God! I know you sent me a ministering angel in the form of that policeman, because when he left, I turned around immediately and the beach was completely abandoned, as empty as it was when I arrived.

There was no sign of the officer; not even his cruiser was in sight. At that moment, I knew God had interceded on my behalf. What's ironic is that the place where I chose to end my life was also, at the time, deserted, lonely and lifeless. Wow, life can be so strange at times. Till this day, I thank the Lord for sparing my life and forgiving me for even contemplating such an awful thing. I composed myself, turned my car around and headed home. That night I began to work on developing a deeper relationship and understanding of God's grace and mercy and how He remains faithful unto us, even when we are yet unfaithful. There is a passage of scripture which states: *"If we are without faith, still He keeps faith, for He will never be untrue to Himself."* —*2 Timothy 2:13*. From that moment on, I believed in Him on another level and trusted Him as never before. In a sense, I had a new lease on life. God saved me from the world and from myself for a divine purpose that would later be revealed. The old saints use to sing a song, "Further along we will know more about it, Further along we will understand why."

For years, the mothers and elders of the church would tell me God had a work for me to do. Although I knew that indeed He did, I continued to struggle and experience a low period in my life. At the end of the day, I was yet stuck with confronting the reality that I had given my all to a man and marriage, and after all my hard work and effort, I was alone. The church services were great and uplifting; however, when the organ stopped and the sermon ended and the saints went back to their respective places, I had to deal with me. So for a period of time, I checked out; I checked out of ministry; I checked out of fellowship; and I checked out of church.

Nine

Moving On

"If I ascend up into heaven, thou art there; if I make my bed in hell, behold thou art there." —Psalm 139:8

Although I had checked out somewhat emotionally from church for a season, I could still hear my father's voice in my spirit saying: "Sybil, the church is the place for you when you are doing well and it's also the place for you when you are not living up to God's standards."

I find where most people get hung up is they stop attending church when they mess up or fall short of the expectations of a Christian. All of us have bad days, weak periods of time. We experience lapses in judgement and sometimes do things we know we shouldn't do. Even if your feet slip to the point of a backslidden condition, the safest place for a backslider is in the House of the Lord. In the Book of Jeremiah 3:14, the prophet lets us know that God is married to the backslider. God never forgets you. You are never out of sight, out of mind. He has already proven He is willing to go to the gates of hell to reclaim His children.

My dad's sound advice rings ever true, especially in this day and time when people attempt to intellectualize and rationalize reasons for not attending church. Church is important! You can't stay effective for Christ, working all the time or sitting at home forsaking prayer and studying. While work is honorable and man should work, it can't be all that we do. For some, working has become a major crutch and top excuse for not attending church, especially in the time of a shaky economy. I don't give my members a hard time or try and scare them into coming to church, but I do let them know that if they ask the Lord to allow them to attend, He will make a way for them. As a result, many have caught on by faith. Some saints refuse to work Sundays, in spite of overtime offers and promotions. Usually, they are the ones who are doing the best financially. It could be just a coincidence, but I doubt it. Notwithstanding, I'm not closed minded to the fact there are some fields of work where it is required to work some Sundays. I simply believe that God will make a way for you to attend church if you press your way. And for so many of us pressing our way today is not like pressing was a generation ago. Just a generation ago, many saints were worse off financially. They had barriers and obstacles that made attending church more difficult. The saints couldn't afford cars and took public transportation. And if the church didn't have a van, they would walk, pressing their way to church. Today, we just jump in our vehicles, and yet we are still late for service and lackadaisical in our efforts. If Jesus did us the way we do Him, I cringe to think about what the outcome of our lives would be.

As the pastor, I get all kinds of ridiculous emails, texts, third-party messages and telephone calls with the strangest reasons, excuses and sometimes lies on why "saints" are missing or absent from service. Excuses ranging from missing dentures to saints' feelings of hypocrisy because they don't believe that their lives line up with the word. But I tell them all to get into the press and make their way to the House of the Lord. Now I know how teachers felt when the students would tell them the dog ate their homework. Conversely, there is no problem too hard for God and there is no situation beyond His ability to handle. So, simply make every effort to get to a service.

My dad knew firsthand the struggles and pains I was enduring. He was a wise man and a dynamic leader, but he was my dad first. He covered me with prayer instead of burying me with judgment. He chose to encourage and did everything in his power to help motivate me. He was concerned about me, the whole person — mind, body, soul and spirit. My father's loyalty extended beyond the four walls of the church. To my dad, there was no such thing as "out of sight, out of mind." He was truly into soul winning and supporting the saints. He shared that agape love and never stooped to the *tit-for-tat* level. His love and service came free of any hidden agenda. Each Sunday he and my mother held their own personal outreach after service. He would have my mother call and see about members who were missing if they had not given an account of their absences. He took his under-shepherd job seriously, demonstrating the willingness and ability to leave the 99 to go back and get the one. Yet, all of his support and all of his love could not save me from myself. There was some hard work that I had to do. I had to pick myself up out of the pit of despair and push ahead. I had to rebuke depression, deny self, look up and live. I was entering into a new chapter of my life; one that I would write and

God would direct. My children and I were in a safe place. We were close to my parents and we were surrounded by prayer. The Lord helped me to successfully detangle myself from the strong grip of emotional and physical abuse. Now I had to strengthen the weak and repair the broken places in my life. There was a process that I had to endure, which was extremely uncomfortable but necessary.

After going through what seemed like months of crying and sorrow, things began to slowly get better. There is a saying that time heals all wounds. Yeah, it may heal them, but there were scars from those wounds. I heard someone frame it as "delivered, but damaged," and for a season that was me. But thanks be to God, I was no longer entangled with the stronghold that had me bound. I started to regain strength and a healthier outlook on life. It was at this point, I decided that I wasn't going to let a couple of bad decisions and adverse situations dictate the rest of my life. I was going to restart what the cares of this life had stalled and attempted to abort. I was determined to take back everything the enemy had stolen from me. What the enemy meant for my evil, God turned into good. Therefore, I committed to going forward and that meant cleaning up the messes and settling unfinished business, starting with going back to school and finishing my college degree. That alone was a major task as an adult, but thanks be to God, I had the help of my family. The support of an amazing family means the world to you when you are going through trying to make drastic life changes. However, I was determined to make a successful life for me and my children. As a result, my focus was on my studies and successfully finishing. Church, during this period of my life, was not my main priority. However, that being said, the Lord remained a constant and central focus of my life.

Now, sometimes I missed the saints because they were such a big part of my life. Notwithstanding, I really didn't miss service that much. I had been in church my whole life so the break allowed me the opportunity to observe the church as an outsider, looking in with a neutral disposition for a season. My dad continued to keep me updated about church activities and functions. Although I was sporadic in my attendance, he always made sure my children could attend if they wanted to — in fact, he insisted that they attend. I knew I had to get back to church.

I started attending and participating more in the ministry. I wouldn't miss a Sunday. However, those services during the week were a challenge. On special occasions, I would make every effort to attend. Every year, most times in June, my dad would have a revival at the church. He believed in revivals to keep the saints on fire for the Lord. He didn't believe in downtime when serving the Lord. Today, we don't have nearly as many revivals as we should. And it is evident, whereas it seems as though saints of God have lost the urgency of salvation and the realization of a soon-coming Savior. As we witness the world drastically changing for the worse, we seem to be more relaxed and less focused.

My dad planned a revival and had a guest evangelist scheduled to speak. I was familiar with the evangelist and respected the anointing that the Lord had on his life. So, I told my dad I would probably come. Something overwhelmed and compelled me to attend. So I went and on the first night the evangelist was amazing. When he spoke, I felt like the Lord was speaking to me directly. The visiting elder preached a message, "I will arise and go home." On that night, the Lord had sent a tailored word for my situation. The message spoke to my condition and my heart. See, I was not like the prodigal son, but in my own way I had allowed the cares of the world to distract and derail my vision and goals. I had become like that church in Ephesus, which John the revelator described as leaving its first love. Life has a way of beating you down if you let it or should I say, accept it. My dad always said, "You don't fall out of fellowship or backslide overnight, it's a gradual process." You lose interest in the things of God or you began to prioritize secular and worldly things ahead of your walk with Christ. Before you know it, you began to lack the desire and/or the will to serve the Lord in the beauty of holiness. Your communication diminishes and you become a citizen of this world. I knew it was time to reconnect with the ministry and serve the Lord like never before. Each week it seemed like life was getting better. I had gotten a new job and my pay had increased tremendously. It was during this time that I met and developed lifelong relationships with two people that helped shape my life for the better. I gained two loyal friends who left an indelible impression on my life: Ellen and my dearly departed Doug, the love of my life. These two great blessings were the rays of sunshine in my life after the bitter rain.

I was introduced to Ellen who became and remains my very best friend to this day. She is no fair-weather friend and there were no hidden agendas in our relationship. But only the Lord can take two strangers from altogether different walks of life with nothing in common and make them sisters in His name. Our relationship started out in the work environment, then transformed. It was completely unexpected, yet life changing. Ellen became my business mentor, sister and friend. Out of all of that, I valued our friendship the most. The Word of God lets us know that *"A friend sticks closer than a brother." —Proverbs 18:24.* Not only did she hire me and teach me the business of childcare, she also allowed me to run a portion of her company. Ellen taught me valuable business lessons that I carry to this day. These lessons even apply in the Kingdom of God. For more than 20 years, He allowed us to work hand-in-hand, helping shape communities through excellent childcare. And through some of the most trying times in my life, Ellen has been a constant — providing me with sage wisdom and sound advice. She is one of the smartest and caring people I have ever met. The times we differed in opinion we never fell out of fellowship or the covenant we developed with one another. We even joined our families, becoming Godparents to each other's children. Though Ellen has moved and we don't see each other as much, my love for her has not diminished one iota. I am forever loyal and committed to her.

Soon after graduation from the education program, I was offered a good paying job working for a prestigious university in the Boston area. Little did I know that this would be a pivotal point in my life; one that would position me for the next move which God had in store for me. My whole world would soon change — my professional and personal life would see new heights. It is fascinating and an incredible blessing to behold the Lord and all His majesty, experiencing how quickly the Lord can change your life around and put you in position to succeed.

I once preached a message called "Suddenly." That's how things happen in the Kingdom of God. Additionally, the Bible talks about how the Lord can just speak things into existence. Things were really looking up for me. I had met a co-worker at Tufts University who was a real gentleman. Actually, he was my Prince Charming, Douglas Anthony Dunwoody. He was a man, a real man. He was big and strong. His hands were not manicured, and he didn't sit behind a desk. His big hands defined and displayed the hard work he did. Mostly, we only made eye contact, but at times we did engage in small talk. At that point in time, I wasn't looking for a man. Jesus was my man and the Holy Ghost was my Comforter. I knew that I would love again, but I was in no big rush. But the Word of God lets us know that: *"Whoso findeth a wife findeth a good thing, and obtaineth favour of the Lord." —Proverbs 18:22*

We were from two totally different religious backgrounds. He was from the Catholic persuasion and me, the Pentecostal church. But much like God, our love transcended everything. He treated me like a man is supposed to treat a woman. He knew how to make a woman feel special. I was his queen and he was most certainly my king. Today so many women are looking for Mr. Right and end up with Mr. Right Now. But for those willing to wait patiently and allow the Lord to do the work for you, God has already prepared your Boaz. God has a man that may not be perfect in your eyes but will be perfect for you in His eyes. Be advised that Prince Charming's come in all different shapes, sizes, colors and all walks of life. Not only do you need to be able to discern things in the spirit, you have to be able to see the good in a man.

Initially, I attempted to keep Doug away from my family. We were getting to know one another and building a relationship. After hiding Doug for a while, the time had come for me to introduce him to my family. I was sure he would be well received from most of the family, but I wasn't exactly sure about my eldest son. However, it really didn't matter because I had chosen this man and he was going to be a part of my life. So whatever issues my eldest son had would be worked out. And it was just like I imagined. Everyone in my family liked him immediately, except for my eldest son. I knew this time I would be okay. I knew that this man made me feel like no other man had ever made me feel. I believe it was that great American Motown singer who we refer to as the Queen of Soul who said, "You make me feel like a natural woman." The way he looked at me, I knew he was sent from God. And what made our relationship greater was that my dad liked him and gave me his vote of confidence. I was a grown woman who had three children and an ex-husband, but my dad's approval was still important to me. We were like good friends. I could tell him things that I couldn't share with anyone. So when my father gave me his okay I felt good about entering this new phase of life.

Doug made me feel safe enough and vulnerable to love again. This was a major piece of my healing. I was still a little leery, but Doug assured me that he loved me and my family and would never hurt us. I believed him, he was so genuine. He was a strong willed, no nonsense man. He could spot a phony a mile away, and before God saved him, Doug did not mind letting people know when they got on his nerves. He had keen discernment when it came to authenticity. I remember one Sunday Doug came to pick me up from church service. Now my family always attended church, but Doug attended when he felt like it and he wasn't going to allow anyone to force him to change. However, this Sunday he was waiting for me outside and one of the brother preachers, whom Doug didn't particularly care for at the church, went outside, approached the car and motioned Doug to roll down the window. I cringed at the notion of what the conversation would be. I hurried to the car to prevent any confrontation. Not that there would be a fight or anything, but Doug would give him a piece of his mind and it wouldn't be filtered through faith or the Holy Ghost. Initially, Doug ignored him and acted as if he didn't see him. So the gentlemen went over and tapped on the window. That was a mistake. As he tried to persuade Doug to come in for service, Doug grew impatient with him and told the elder (words I can't repeat) to get away from him. I was mortified. My only saving grace was that the man was hard of hearing and behaved as though he didn't hear Doug. I begged Doug not to repeat it. Being the loving husband he was, he acquiesced to my request. A fall-out of that magnitude could have been a disaster. Disagreements in church tend to be magnified. But I think deep down inside the brother may not have quite understood what Doug said, but he got the gist of it. Doug was a strong willed man and didn't have anything to prove. He just didn't tolerate foolishness. After that incident, I knew the Lord was going to save Doug. He had character and integrity that backed up his strong will. He had some strong core beliefs and values that made him easy to read. There was no pretense with him.

Consequently, before the Lord saved Doug, he drank, smoked and cursed, in that order. But he consciously kept all of that negativity away from me. He would drink his beer in the car. He never brought that stuff into the house. He respected and honored me as his wife and as his pastor. And when the Lord did save him, he kept that strong will and used it in the service of the Lord. My God saved Doug and it was a marvelous work. Shortly after Doug gave his life to the Lord and began his service, the Lord called my dad home, and boy did I need Doug for this traumatic loss in my life.

Ten

Organizing the Right Team

"It was He who gave some to be apostles, some to be prophets, some to be evangelists, and some to be pastors and teachers, to prepare God's people for works of service, so that the body of Christ may be built up." —Ephesians 4:11-12

When my dad died, it was really hard to believe he was gone. I guess I was somewhat delusional, trying to convince myself that it wasn't real and perhaps a bad dream — until they lowered him into the ground. The inevitable had finally come. I could no longer deny or block out his passing. As I began to breathe in the stale air of the Oak Lawn Cemetery, the smell of death surrounded me; and as the foggy mist pitter-pattered on my face, the cold harsh reality that had so easily escaped me had finally sunk in. My dad, the man that was larger than life to me, had transitioned to glory. My Superman had turned in his cape for a crown of righteousness. My earthly hero had now become the newest member of my greater cloud of witnesses. No longer would I enjoy the pleasure of hearing him say, "*Sybil.*" Oh how I loved to hear him call my name. There was such comfort and care in his calling.

As the saints started placing the flowers onto his casket, I could feel every rose as it hit. The thud each flower made pierced my eardrum. It felt like a knife wound penetrating my heart. Incredible grief began to overtake me. All I wanted to do was fall out and roll all over the grass, yelling and screaming, "*Why Lord, Why now Lord, Why me, Lord?*" But not so, I couldn't act in that manner; one, it would be unseemly; two, and more importantly, my father wouldn't want that, and I was determined to honor his memory in every way. He expected me to act like the leader he saw in me and the leader the Lord called me to be. We would gather together for his Home-Going Celebration, and I know he was counting on me to step right in and assume the mantle. The church members' well-being and salvation were in the balance. There was no time for excessive grieving or lack of focus. Besides, not only was I his natural daughter, I was his spiritual Elisha and he was my spiritual Elijah. I had gone through modern day Gilgal with him, and I was there when the Lord took him up. I was positioned in the right place at the right time. It was me whom the Lord told my dad that I would be the Joshua to his Moses. Before me stood a great assignment! Favorably, for me and the members of the church my dad had done what most competent leaders do: putting into place a succession plan and the proper instructions for the ministry to carry out the work of the Lord. His forward thinking helped to make the transition as smooth as it could be given the culture shock we were experiencing. He did his best to warn me about what to watch out for and gave me an outline of the possible obstacles and hurdles we would face. Notwithstanding all his warnings, he could only tell me so much and guide me so far. I had to face the future perils on my own. I had to lean on the Lord for my understanding and guidance. In spite of all the guidance and preparation, we couldn't avoid the obvious; my father's dying created a new paradigm, a new era and a new move for Little Zion Church of God in Christ.

Me, Sybil Faye Darby Dunwoody, a woman, would now be at the helm of the church. There was no time to practice or work out the kinks; it was prime time now, a new beginning.

The pastor is a key figure in both your spiritual and natural life, so this loss was devastating. Now I was the

Pastor of the church and the new under-shepherd of the flock. I was no longer Sybil or Evangelist Missionary Dunwoody, I was Pastor Dunwoody. I was expected to be a rock. It was no time for on the job training. I had to hit the ground running. There was a steep learning curve and only through faith would I be able to step right into position. It was my voice and my spirit that the people would now follow, and no one wants to follow a cry baby or perceived weakling. That's all the doubters needed to see or hear. They already questioned my leadership and saw me as the misguided, weaker vessel unable to lead dispassionately. Regardless, soon the brotherhood found out that this tenderhearted, gentle and even vulnerable Pastor Sybil Dunwoody could battle and conduct spiritual warfare with the best of them, all while wearing a mean St. John suit and some Manolo Blahnik four inch heels.

Church people expect and want their leaders to be rocks, super-human beings of fortitude. They also want their leaders to look good while doing it. Lord knows I had no problem with that. Unfortunately, some called it vanity. However, I believed then and to this day, that I bring my best before the Lord — both inwardly and with my outer appearance. Furthermore, I did so with strength, determination and complete composure. Besides, who wants a leader who is unable to maintain self-control in the midst of crisis and trauma? The answer, no one! Christians are not supposed to grieve like the unbelievers, for we know that those that die in Christ simply sleep away. We know that to be absent from the body is to be present with the Lord. My dad, in dying, was in a better position than all of us left here still trying to work out our soul salvation. Let me tell you it was most certainly a "workout." Anyways with leadership comes responsibility. Although members sometimes put unrealistic expectations on their leaders; nonetheless, "It is what it is," and my crying had to be in private. I had to be a big girl, strong in the Lord and very courageous. I didn't feel like it all the time but as the saying goes, "Faith it till you make it." And that is just what I did.

While going through this tremendous ordeal, I heard the voice of the Lord speak to me similarly as He spoke to Joshua when He said: "Moses my servant is dead. As I was with James, so shall I be with you Sybil. I will never leave you nor forsake you." That was the blessed assurance I needed. I was the one God called to lead the church into the next move; therefore, I knew God would provide the guidance and direction. I didn't know how He would do it, I just knew He would. Members were looking to me for strength and encouragement. Little did they know that most days I needed it more than they did. But that was okay because we all were journeying down new territory. We were travelling on unchartered waters. But one thing I was sure of was that if we kept our eyes and mind stayed on Jesus, we would not sink nor would we self-destruct. It didn't matter how rough the waters got as long as our central focus and goal was Christ and Him crucified, we would surely make it.

Yeah, we were making traumatic changes; and yeah, change was difficult, but God was building character in us. Plus those old saints wanted to see if I was the little spoiled girl which so many of them pegged me to be. Furthermore, they really wanted to see if I had the intestinal fortitude to divest myself from my former position and operate in my new capacity. By man, I was known for my stylish wardrobe, but God knew my heart. Sometimes you are so misunderstood. Clothes never made me, God's anointing made me. But those that had labored in the ministry wondered would Sybil step up with the holy boldness and faith it was going to take to shepherd a flock of people who just lost a giant of a leader who was so many things to so many people. No, I couldn't but the Christ in me could. Maybe that's why I attached myself to *Philippians 4:13:* *"I can do all things through Christ, Who strengthens me."* I knew all eyes were on me and I had to rise above expectations, not for the purposes of being right but rather for the assurance that the anointing would continue to flow. Saints would continue to be delivered; and the work of the Lord would continue with uncompromising integrity. Therefore, any suffering I did needed to be done in silence and private. I had to keep my emotions in control, although deep down inside I was in complete turmoil. I had to forgo major weeping and mourning to keep my church moving and vital. I had to endure the foolish phone calls by some who thought they knew the word of God but quoted the scriptures out of context. These were the same ones who thought they didn't need to come to Bible class or study the scriptures.

It is amazing the amount of time we waste going through the motions and rituals. The Kingdom of God is serious business and the time for the "same ole same ole" or "that will do" spirits had to be bound and cast out of our midst. Equally important, I had to organize a team that could help me move the church in the direction that the Lord called us. Drastic steps had to be taken for the ministry's well-being. Meanwhile in the midst of all of this change, I had to remember that I was a wife and that call was my first duty. I had to focus on my marriage and being the wife my husband wanted me to be. My husband hadn't signed up for all of the responsibility that the Lord had placed upon me. We had planned to live a simple life, travel and grow old together, enjoying one another's company. Our children were adults so we only had to focus on each other. We were entering a new era of our lives. My husband didn't sign on to share me with 200 other people. My new role as pastor was going to have a dramatic effect on his life. Was he really ready for the 2:00 a.m. phone calls, the late night trips to the hospital or police station or wherever I needed to be for the saints of God? This new assignment tested the strength of our union. And to be completely honest, I wasn't sure we were going to make it. But the Lord was on our side and honored and prospered our marriage.

I had learned numerous lessons from my dad about team building. He was a great mentor to so many preachers. I witnessed first-hand the multi-faceted relationship building that the leader develops with his people. I learned what to do, but more importantly, I learned what not to do. There were many people in the midst that were part of the ministry, but sadly their loyalty was more to my father, as opposed to the ministry of the church that he dedicated his life to. So I had to tread on water and sort through the committed and the posers. A small faction of the church was stooped in tradition and couldn't fathom the idea of me, a woman, leading the church. Even my mother, the late, great Carolyn Darby, had questions about my leadership. This whole concept of a woman leading was new to her. Notwithstanding, she was 100 percent in my corner and gave me and the ministry her undying support.

Everyone on my team had to be courageous, fully persuaded and committed to the Kingdom of God and me. They needed to be independent thinkers, who would in the final analysis condescend to my leadership and decisions knowing that God called me to lead and watch for their souls. A team is worthless if all they do is "yes" you to death. "Yes men" and "yes women" would be detrimental to my leadership and the ministry. I wasn't going to elevate someone just because they worked in the ministry prior to my father's death. The primary reason was because I had a unique understanding of the inner workings of the ministry and understood the secret battles and issues my dad had to deal with. Some people worked in certain capacities of the ministries — not necessarily for the right reasons; and some people jockeyed for positions for selfish motives. They were happy about the new changes because they believed that this new move presented opportunity for a power grab.

Church people are human first and have frailties like everyone else; and unless we are rigid with our depravities, we can make some terrible decisions that can hurt a ministry to the core. We all have ideas and goals, but they must line up with the leader's vision. A house divided against itself cannot stand. The anointing flows with unity. The strongest saints are the obedient ones. We were conducting spiritual warfare and my team had to be battle tested. When you are fighting spiritual wickedness in high places, weak and impotent saints are not going to cut it. Lackadaisical saints with a laissez-faire attitude were more hurtful than helpful. Only passionate people with a strong conviction and desire to advance the Kingdom would be members of the team. As I consulted the Lord, He strategically placed people in their proper positions.

While simultaneously building a new team to lead the ministry forward, I had to deal with the unsettled, disgruntled faction of the ministry that had plans of their own, which didn't include me at the helm. This small group of members was not sold on the idea of my being pastor. They had other candidates in mind. Being in the ministry all my life, I have seen several church splits. None of them ever ended well. A small group of contrary spirits can stir up chaos that could divide a ministry and lead to destruction. I knew it was important to be wise, methodic and spirit led. While they were operating secretly, I had to operate above them.

I reflected on the Apostle Paul's first letter to the church at Corinth when he told them: *"For God is not the author of confusion, but of peace, as in all churches of the saints."* *—1 Corinthians 14:33.* I was determined not to let Little Zion turn into Lodebar. Lodebar was an awful place where the Spirit of the Lord didn't dwell. The worst thing to have is a church without the Spirit of the Lord and just a building. I was fasting, praying and watching. This ministry had birthed numerous churches and great miracles were performed in our midst; and there was no devil in hell that was going to disrupt, distract or destroy us. We were a prayed-up church which the Lord built, and like the Apostle Peter's confession I declared that: *"Upon the Rock of Jesus, Little Zion's Church was built and neither the gates of hell nor some imps of Satan would prevail against it."* So, those haters waited with bated breath at the demise of the church. One was quoted saying: "Don't nobody want to sit under a woman! God ain't called women to preach and pastor." Another one was quoted as saying "I'll give them six months and they will be closed down." Sadly, some of these main rabble rousers were the most faithful members under my dad's leadership. Given their loyalty to my dad, I expected that they would at least give me a chance and rally behind me for his sake; the church they professed to love. Boy was I wrong, which just goes to show that some people are able to compartmentalize their faith. They were able to act perniciously in one manner and dance and shout around the church the next. This was utter hypocrisy. They began to exercise what I called demonic boldness; we sometimes call them "talking back demons." Those are the ones that must be confronted and exposed.

Deep inside I was really hurt and actually felt sorry for some of them. These people had allowed the devil to use them in such an ugly manner, and they didn't even realize that they were the enemy's pawns. Because of what I have witnessed, I am so careful to keep the saints — especially the new converts — grounded, humbled and prayerful. If you are not surefooted in the Word of God and in constant relationship and communion with the Lord, you can be easily fooled.

My first two position assignments were my co-assistants. These positions had to be filled by people that I could trust. The first individual I had known for more than twenty years. She worked tirelessly for the ministry. My father called her his songbird. Her voice was angelic; she could move a church to tears as she sang under the anointing. But even more than her beautiful melodious voice, she had a praying spirit. She could get a prayer through. She prayed in tongues and lived the life. The Lord assured me she would be loyal and would not harm me. Loyalty was big to me. Disloyalty was a disqualifier. The second individual He gave me as an assistant was a young man in the ministry but full of fervor and a pure heart. He was just a good man and someone I knew would also be loyal to me unto death. These two were my eyes and ears. They served me with integrity and excellence, and I demanded nothing less.

Eleven

Sometimes They Leave

"They went out from us, but they did not really belong to us. For if they had belonged to us, they would have remained with us; but their going showed that none of them belonged to us."
—*1 John 2:19*

Sometimes they leave because they want to. They make up their minds that it's time to move on. They say things like "The church isn't the same anymore" or "I don't feel the love I used to" or even "The church seems to be all about finances and every time I go they are asking for money," etc., etc. If you have been around ministry for a period of time, I'm sure you have heard them all as well.

Sometimes they leave because they need to or should I say they believe they need to move on. They may give reasons such as, "I got a word from the Lord." Consequently, in some cases they did receive a word from the Lord; but even in those cases, it would be beneficial for them to consult the pastor for confirmation. However, I never held any hard feelings against them, for some had a strong desire to start their own ministry work or serve in another capacity. Regardless, I understand and pray for them.

Sometimes they leave because they feel they have to. They may have acted in an unseemly manner and embarrassed themselves or the church; or they may have been caught or exposed in a compromising situation and believe they can't stay and face the consequences. All kinds of actions fit in this category, but I'll let your imagination help you figure out the possibilities. All that being said the bottom line is that people leave.

Most of the time when they leave it's neither good nor bad but rather necessary. The majority of the time it's in God's will, but a portion of the time it's in the person's will. Either way, they are gone and they are no longer laboring with you in the vineyard.

Initially, I had a hard time with people leaving. First of all, I believe every person is valuable to God in His Kingdom. My heart hurt for most of the souls that left because they were a part of me. One day, during a period of time when it seemed as though a lot of people were leaving the church, the Lord brought to my remembrance a conversation I had with my dad early in his ministry. I was asking him why did this person leave and why did that person leave? These people had stood up and testified that they were lifelong members of the church and openly professed their love for the church and my dad. Then he said something profound to me: "Sybil, you need to understand sometimes people in ministry are like scaffolding." "Scaffolding," I said. He said, "Yes, scaffolding." And he went on to explain scaffolding is equipment that builders use when they are repairing or building something. He said that in ministry there are some people who will be with you for a season and then they will leave. It doesn't have anything to do with you personally; it's just the fact that God sent them to you for a specific purpose. Don't be remiss because some of the folks who said they were in it for the long haul and would never leave, gave and received what they were supposed to and moved on.

Consequently, the leaving I experienced seemed to be different. While I know ministry is not personal, it was most definitely different in my eyes. People seemed to be leaving over what I thought were petty issues. With a church practically on every corner in the city, people have a smorgasbord of ministries to choose from. So the moment they hear something they don't like at one church, they can move on down the street. As a leader, it is incumbent upon you to understand when a person or family joins your church there is something special that draws them to your church. Some people join because they love the singing and praise. Some join for the love they feel from the saints, one to another. Others join for the preached Word. They heard a Word from the Lord that sparked their heart and the Spirit led them to connect with you. Then there is another set of people who joined because Mama, Big Daddy and Cousin Johnnie are members, and your church is their family church.

So, why do they leave? Well, first of all everyone that comes to your church has a story and a past. All have issues, whether big or small, which they are dealing with, and the reality is that some join for the wrong reasons. Therefore, they leave because during their time in membership, something happens that causes a slight or hard feelings. A trigger occurs, such as someone felt that the pastor preached a message about him or her specifically. They say things like "Pastor Dunwoody was preaching on me;" or "Pastor Dunwoody didn't go to the hospital to visit my mother." They also say, "I pay my tithes to the church and I couldn't get help with my light bill." Usually, if we have any money in the church treasury, we will help members. However, sometimes we just don't have it, and in those rare cases, people leave with hurt feelings.

As I have previously stated, some members want you to be not only their personal pastor but also everything else to them. And there is only so much I can do as a leader. Notwithstanding, I like to let people know that often-times deliverance and blessings are tied to obedience to God and those whom have rule over them. *"Have confidence in your leaders and submit to their authority, because they keep watch over you as those who must give an account. Do this so that their work will be a joy, not a burden, for that would be of no benefit to you."* —*Hebrews 13:17.* However, my responsibility is not to lord my position over them, nor should I intimidate or manipulate the saints. My role is to protect and correct, not for the purpose of humiliation but for the purpose of pleasing God. When the saints do wrong, I always attempt to correct them with lovingkindness. Some people who join are not sure-footed in ministry or stable and don't allow themselves to be rooted in a ministry. Therefore, they are moved by every whim and doctrine. Regardless, they are still important to me and I hurt when they leave. It took me some time to learn how to deal with people leaving. Irrespective of the knowledge I had, on some occasions I still took it personally when people left. I wondered if there was something I could have done for them to continue on with me. Was it something I said or did? Sometimes it was — or should I say, it was the Christ in me. However, I always tried to preach, "What Thus Saith the Lord." and not "What Thus Saith Sybil." Because if I preach, "Thus Saith the Lord," and it hurts or upsets someone, they must take their hard feelings and grievances to the Lord. On the other hand, if I preach, "Thus saith Sybil," then I am never too big to apologize. And if people are not satisfied and still want to leave, I give them my blessing as long as they leave appropriately.

Where problems arise is when people leave and they make up stories (lies) about me or my church. It's unfortunate that it happens, but it does. I never set out to hurt anyone, even the troublemakers; however, I can't say I'm not glad when they leave. But sometimes the ones that leave are the closest to you, and it only makes it difficult. Nevertheless, you have to prepare and move on; the ministry and the work of the Lord must continue. Sometimes you just have to love some folks from a distance.

Twelve

We Are Just The Vessels

"And He said unto me, My grace is sufficient for thee: for My strength is made perfect in weakness. Most gladly therefore will I rather glory in my infirmities, that the power of Christ may rest upon me." —2 Corinthians 12:9

The quotation above is a familiar passage of scripture which involves the Apostle Paul, arguably the greatest evangelist that ever lived. The Apostle Paul was given honor, recognition and revelation from God comparable to no man. He describes being taken into the highest and innermost places of God. He was carried up into the third heaven, which is paradise; and because of this great revelation and experience, he was given a thorn in his flesh and buffeted by a messenger of Satan. This thorn in his flesh troubled the Apostle Paul. He desperately wanted to be delivered from this condition. The Bible, nor the Apostle himself, never defined what that condition or affliction was but referred to it as a "thorn in his flesh." Till this day, Biblical scholars and teachers speculate about the "thorn," but only God and Paul knew what that affliction was.

However, Paul in his second letter to the church at Corinth shares with the readers his communication he had with the Lord. He shares the experience of how he went to God three times requesting that the Lord remove this thorn from his flesh. It is at that point which the Lord assures Paul that His (God's) grace is sufficient for him. God's grace is defined as the unmerited favor and His unconditional love. It's not due to any miraculous power or superfluous intellect we possess, but it's God's decision to love and favor us in spite of ourselves. So when God spoke those words (My Grace is Sufficient) to Paul, Paul was clear and knew that it was God's will for him to endure this thorn. Further, the Apostle shares the revelation by which he states he received this thorn: that he might remain humble, given all the anointing he was endowed and all the supernatural encounters he enjoyed with God.

Paul's life in the Kingdom of God serves as a record to all who work in ministry and struggle with the "what if's." What if I was 100 percent healthy? What if the church treasury was filled and overloaded? What if the church had 200 more members? What if? What if? What if? So often the "what if's" become excuses for not excelling in ministry. The Apostle Paul took his "what if" to God and was reassured that God's grace was sufficient.

Everyone serving God be advised that the greater the anointing, the greater the suffering you must endure. The world has an economic theory which states, "There is no such thing as a free lunch;" meaning somehow you pay for it. Likewise, in the Kingdom of God, there is no such thing as a free anointing; therefore, you must be prepared to endure a certain level of suffering. I admonish you to never covet another person's anointing but work with what God has given you in a Spirit of faith, integrity and excellence. And, in doing so, God will do "it" for you, whatever that "it" is. I strongly believe that at some point everyone who works in ministry will have a similar conversation with God. Upon your endowment of God's anointing, you too, will be given a thorn in your flesh or the thorn already dwelling in you (being dormant), will rise. You, too, will suffer with a perceived hindrance. So often many of us, with our strong desire to serve and please God, strive to be perfect beings in our service to Him; but none are perfect but the Father.

We want perfect health, superior wisdom and super abundant bank accounts, etc.; partially based in carnality. These things offer a false sense of confidence that given we can do a greater work for God. We, the called, do not have to put our hope in anything. We must have the conviction and disposition of: *"Being confident of this very thing, that He which hath begun a good work in you will perform it until the day of Jesus Christ."* —Philippians 1:6. And know with blessed assurance the grace that God gives each of us will allow us to endure any challenges which we face. Yes, all are good and beneficial when used for intended purposes. But they don't determine how effective you will be in your ministry. Yes, resources are valuable when winning souls, and he that winneth souls must be wise. But it's not the external or carnal things that make the difference, but rather it's the Spirit of God and His grace that transforms lives.

Every thorn in your life is not going to be removed. Some similar to those of Paul are thorns designed to keep us humble and at the feet of Jesus. Some are there to increase your prayer life and some are there to protect you from that inner you which gives space for ego and arrogance. When you serve and live for Christ, the enemy is determined to destroy your fellowship.

Anyone who tells you that the thorn wasn't removed because of your faith is advising you in error and speaking words of discouragement into your life. I understand and share some of the same beliefs as my co-laborers in the Word of Faith movement. I believe that too many saints lack the faith to serve God in the capacity by which they have been called. However, I am clear that in some situations and circumstances, we must suffer and endure as good soldiers for the cause of Christ. Yes, He can heal, deliver and set free. Notwithstanding, some people will see Him, having died with afflictions in their bodies. But if the Spirit of the Lord is in you, hypertension, diabetes, cancer, HIV, AIDS, and any other sicknesses you can name, are just words.

If we want and have been called to serve God, there is no limitation on us. God is made strong through our infirmities and the thorns in our flesh. That is why He says, *"Let the weak say I am strong and the poor say I am rich."* —*Joel 3:10*. As long as we are certain that it is never us completing the work, but rather the Christ in us, we shall be fine. I remember early in my ministry, I was somewhat conflicted in the praying and laying hands on the sick. I never had an issue praying for salvation, restoration and reconciliation. I was confident and excited about praying for the saints' success in all areas of their lives. However, in praying for sickness in the body, I wasn't as strong as I felt I should have been. I knew God could use whom He chose, and that God could heal all maladies of man.

For a period of time I felt uncomfortable praying for others' healing when I was sick in my body. The sickness of diabetes had attacked my body, and besides doing damage to the physical body, I allowed it to affect my spiritual being. It made me feel uneasy praying for others when I needed healing. Soon it became increasingly difficult as more of the saints requested prayer for healing. One after another let me know what they were suffering with and requested I touch and agree with them for their healing.

So much like Paul, I sought the Lord and asked Him to heal me from this disease; this proverbial "thorn in my flesh" which I believed was hindering me from praying for the sick. I asked the Lord to heal me or at least give me the courage and conviction to pray for the sick. He never answered the request, so I increased my prayer and private time with the Lord, seeking Him like never before. What I needed was a Word from the

Lord. So often the enemy, who constantly works to distract and derail our spiritual progress, takes our focus off the bigger picture and bogs us down with the mundane. The bottom line is that God can heal and deliver anyone from anything. In addition, He uses whomever He chooses. He uses any instrument, any person or any situation for His glory — not ours.

One Sunday morning during our worship service, we witnessed an unusual move of the Spirit of God. It wasn't unusual for the Spirit of God to flow in our midst, but this move differed from what we had seen. The Spirit of the Lord was high, and the Lord was troubling the waters and something special would occur this day. I had glanced out in the congregation and my eyes came upon a relative I hadn't seen in a while. She wasn't an official member of the church but she visited occasionally. I was so glad to see her. I knew she had been dealing with some very serious health issues, and I had been lifting her up in prayer. Sometimes in life you need more than deliverance; you need a miracle from the Lord. After I preached my sermon, it was customary to call a prayer line by which members and guests in need would usually come to the altar and receive individual prayer.

My relative entered the prayer line, and as she approached the altar, I laid my hands on her and prayed under the anointing. While in the midst of praying, the Spirit of the Lord spoke and said, "She is healed." I was amazed, given what she was suffering with. Not amazed that God can heal because I know God can heal anything, but rather I had never before heard of anyone being healed from this horrific disease. At the same time, another pastor within the city called my church and asked if this particular woman was attending service with us. He stated that in the midst of his worship service the Lord spoke to him and said this woman was healed. I was amazed at the work of the Lord. It was unfathomable. God truly works in mysterious ways. A few days later I received a call from my relative. She was overwhelmed with joy. She told me that during the worship service, while I was praying for her, the Lord told her she had been healed. She stated that she had gone to see her primary care physician, who ran a series of tests. The results he gave her were that she was well. Her T-cell count was higher than that of her doctor's. See she had been diagnosed with HIV-AIDS (when AIDS was a death sentence). But the Lord had healed her. And the more amazing thing is that He used me as the vessel. It was at this point where I truly had a deeper understanding about the context and value of the Apostle Paul's exhortation of God's grace being sufficient. I understood how His strength is made perfect in my weakness.

Now, as an addendum to her testimony, the medical profession states there is no cure for HIV and AIDS. They have stated that the virus is dormant in the body and that my relative still carries the virus. She remains healthy — some 17 years later — and stands on the declaration that God healed her. She ministers around the country letting people know that God can heal all maladies of the mind, body, spirit and soul. God used this yielded vessel, marred by life and life's circumstances, to get the glory and show forth His miracle working power.

We just use the earthly temples that house us. Now that doesn't mean we should act irresponsible with these temples He has given us. It is our responsibility to care for these bodies, primarily because the Spirit of the Lord dwells on the inside. In our lives, just as in my relative's life, God is in control. Once committed to Him, we are no longer our own but have been brought with a price. Paul in his first letter to Timothy described it this way:

"For there is one God and one mediator between God and men, the man Christ Jesus, who gave himself as a ransom for all men — the testimony given in its proper time." —1 Timothy 2:5

Thirteen

Delivered From Dogma And Dysfunction

"But as for you, ye thought evil against me; but God meant it unto good, to bring to pass, as it is this day, to save much people alive." —Genesis 50:20

Whenever you are looking to do something big for God, the enemy's creativity and propensity to wreak havoc and cause confusion in your life is elevated to new levels. It's hard work living saved, let alone trying to work in the Kingdom. Kingdom work is not for the faint of heart or complacent. Be willing to take risks — but not be a risk taker. Be careful to never assume because you are doing the right thing and you have clean and pure motives that everyone will support and encourage you. Sometimes you will be criticized for doing the right thing. There will always be naysayers, complainers and vision distracters. These recalcitrant malcontents, most of whom are impotent spiritually and nearly void of salvation, have a demonic assignment to sow seeds of discords. Because of their perfidiousness, they have succumbed to the wiles of the adversary, becoming pawns of his dastardly plan to derail Kingdom advancement. Because of their sin and disobedience, they are bound and relegated to wander aimlessly through the wilderness of life. There is an old saying that misery loves company; misery breeds contempt and stifles progress. When doing Kingdom work, misery is infectious and, if unchecked, becomes a hindrance to all it comes in contact with. Some will hate you and your anointing for no good reason. Some will envy the move of God in your life and will seek to discredit you and your authority. Chalk it up to spiritual wickedness in high places; but be confident that God has allowed this process for your growth and development. The word of God tells us: *"Beloved, think it not strange concerning the fiery trial which is to try you, as though some strange thing happened unto you:"* —*1 Peter 4:12.*

When I became the pastor of the church, I had a strong belief that some, if not all of the leaders in my jurisdiction, were not in favor of my appointment. Many would have been fine if I just walked away from the fellowship. Now I don't believe that they wished me any harm; however, I was the metaphorical thorn in their side. Heaven only knows how many times they went to

God praying for my removal. And I say that only half-jokingly. Me, the woman, who should have let one of the brother preachers take over and run the church. "A woman ain't got any business over a man" came whispers from the crowd; probably some of the same ones who were in the lineage of those who said "Give us Barabbas." Many believed that my role was one of support and not leadership, especially over men. So had I submitted to their will and went along with their program, as opposed to the will of God, I would have been much less of a threat. I would have been welcomed with open arms had I acquiesced and condescended to my place, or should I say the proverbial place they thought I should have been. Things would have been so much easier for everyone, except the person most affected — me.

My naiveté didn't allow me to expect years of tradition to change overnight because God called me. I was a 21st century trailblazer in one sense; however, I was very aware of great women that came before me and silently worked in prayer to shatter that glass ceiling in ministry. Great women who led churches, without the title of pastor, had laid the foundation for me. I believed that my leading the church represented a new ministry paradigm for our denomination. I was most certain there would be an adjustment period. Just how long that period would be was the million dollar question. All of these people knew me and my family; I was no stranger to them. But as I reflected on the whole scenario, God had transformed me into a new vessel — Sybil was changed to Pastor. He gave me a new name and it was not shepherdess. I was Pastor and I had to respond to the call.

Much of the resistance came from those I worked with. Supporting their visions and ministries with my blood, sweat, tears and money for years meant nothing. I was the outcast trying to change the status quo. However, whether it was intentionally or unintentionally some people sought to kill my influence and will to lead. Through covert backdoor deals, they grinned behind my back and excluded me from the key pivotal meeting and decision making. In addition, they discredited my spiritual appointment and God-given assignment. I understood the mindset because until my dad had evolved in his thinking, he shared some of the same views about women preachers. However, he was never a hindrance and welcomed them to speak at the church. Notwithstanding, I am sure when the Lord spoke to him concerning a woman leading the ministry, it probably helped a little bit that I was his daughter. It is still amazing how some staunch religious people believe every word of the Bible until faced with something to which they have a strong personal disagreement. Those are the most dangerous people because in actuality what they are saying, in so many words, is that they know the situation better than God. What arrogance! That mindset is the purest form of hypocrisy. If we claim to be led by God, then we should be led all of the time — especially during the difficult and uncomfortable times, not when it is convenient for us.

When facing adversity and difficult obstacles, it's hard to imagine what you are enduring is really for your good. Some preach the gospel that once in Christ you don't struggle; however, that is false doctrine. Jesus, being the Son of God and being filled with the Holy Ghost, had struggles and dealt with political perversion. The scriptures let us know that: *"Forasmuch then as Christ hath suffered for us in the flesh, arm yourselves likewise with the same mind: for he that hath suffered in the flesh hath ceased from sin." —1 Peter 4:1.* I expected and prepared for such challenges. I endured the comments from the spiritual peanut gallery. My dad often quoted the scripture,

"Where much is given much is required." —*Luke 12:48.* Therefore, I had to endure, like a good soldier, the ridicule, the passive aggressive attacks and the covert exercises of a group whose spiritual thinking had yet to advance. Given the situation, I had to continue with my assignment. Everything that happened in the infancy of my ministry was allowed or sanctioned by God. Every action and situation fulfilled a purpose. I knew the purpose and learned from it. I had to elevate my thinking and operate in a strategic manner. But was all of this worth it to serve God? Yes, it was! The people I was in a dysfunctional relationship with molded me into the person I am today. All of the criticism, cavalier behavior and sometimes snares only made me a better leader. I learned the valuable lesson that the scripture proclaims which states: *"Then He answered and spake unto me, saying, This is the word of the Lord unto Zerubbabel, saying, Not by might, nor by power, but by my spirit, saith the Lord of hosts."* —*Zechariah 4:6.* The treatment I endured to be a part of something that I helped maintained was far too much work and way too time consuming.

Walking on eggshells and trying not to rock the boat became way too counterproductive. I tolerated the disrespect (when I could) because initially I believed there was a greater good. However, when the lack of respect spilled over to my staff and had potentially negative effects on their ministry, it was time to put a stop to the nonsense. As the spiritual leader and God's under-shepherd to a flock of people, I was their covering and spiritual protection. I had to be strong and relevant for them. So I dealt with the negative treatment and just accepted it as the cost of doing business for the Kingdom of God. My church family was not so willing; however, they put up strong resistance and hated attending jurisdiction meeting but acquiesced to support me. Having to sit in the section delegated for the women's department and not the section reserved for the pastors, my supposed colleagues, I tolerated. Being called a "shepherdess" although "shepherdess" is nowhere in the Bible, and "shepherd mother" as opposed to a pastor, I tolerated. But acting surreptitiously to my ministerial staff and team, who were working to advance in the Kingdom was the final straw. I had to draw the line and decide what was best for me as the leader and what was best to move my church to the next level.

To many of the new members, a lot of the traditions were silly. They were new to the church experience and many had just been delivered from major afflictions and diseases. They were hungry for the word and annoyed with all the pomp and circumstances. After just being delivered from heroin and seeing the miraculous move of God, they didn't have time for outdated traditions of man which had no real root in scripture. These new converts had a zeal that couldn't be contained. It was my duty and responsibility to protect and nurture their young spirits.

Anyone who has served in ministry knows that church can be a dangerous place. There is a saying that: "No wounds hurt worse than the ones inflicted in the House of the Lord." Having been in church my whole life, I had seen firsthand the effects of being wounded in the House of the Lord. Notwithstanding, I had to walk a fine line because, although so many of the new members strongly disliked the pomp and circumstance and the actions of the organization that seemed to disrespect me, that organization was part of my training and development. Given that my thinking had evolved and I was modern in my way of serving the Lord, I was an anomaly being — a woman at the helm.

However, their ideology, no matter how dysfunctional, remained familiar. With all the idiosyncrasies and trivial players, there was still greatness in the foundation. But true greatness was in God. And sometimes you have to leave the familiar comfort and safety of the known. Realistically, I knew that although my dad had made his wishes known and informed the jurisdiction members who supervised him, that I would assume the role of pastor, that didn't make it a done deal in their eyes. Some, trying to seek what they saw as a common ground, posed a co-leadership team, but neither the proposed person nor myself would compromise to such a thing.

I knew that the struggles in my church would be small compared to those I would confront in the jurisdiction. It's amazing how people can change their allegiance to you when you stand in a way they don't agree with. Yeah, I was doing something that was foreign in their eyes, but I was naïve enough to believe that because it was done in the name of the Lord, people would accept it. God had delivered me from one abusive relationship; now I was dead center in the midst of another one. This one was worse on some level because these served God and guarded the souls of men and women. In the early days of our ministry, we would sing an old song which said, "God delivered me. Why should I be bound?" I repeat that song to the saints in my church now.

When God brings you out of something, don't go back, don't even look back. Some of these old songs are so appropriate for today's walk with the Lord. The simplicity of serving God is more amazing than the dramatic awesomeness that we look for today. There is nothing more amazing than resurrection! We need only to reflect on that and get happy, for without The Resurrection we are a people most miserable — absent of hope.

The way the leadership treated and spoke was beyond unfair. Some of the underhanded acts which the people did in the Jurisdiction shouldn't even be mentioned. I remember the old mothers used to talk about the scripture, "*spiritual wickedness in high places*" and refer to the bishops. After careful consideration and intensive prayer and meditation, I tendered my resignation to the Bishop. It was difficult because my whole life of ministry starting with salvation was connected to the Church of God in Christ. However, any relationship that is unhealthy and non-conducive to growth must either be resolved or dissolved. So many people spend way too much time involved in bad, toxic relationships out of convenience. But the unseen damage that grows and festers below the surface forms a malignancy that destroys the soul.

It was time for me to take the ministry to new terrain. Leaving was one of the toughest decisions I ever had to make. However, not only was it the right thing to do, it was the only thing to do. My spiritual growth was in jeopardy and my ability to lead my church successfully was at risk. The dysfunctional relationship I struggled to survive had advanced beyond tolerable into unendurable. Early in my ministry, I preached a message about "Breaking traditions to be blessed." That message was so appropriate for my departure. They teach you when training in ministry that the message is first to the preacher then to the people; meaning that whatever message God inspires within you applies in your life as well. Often preachers of today are so busy telling the people what they need to do that sometimes they neglect to focus on what they themselves need to do. That's why I believe it's so important to preach what God gives you and not your personal commentary. And when your personal commentary overtakes the message, let the congregation know.

I had matured spiritually and the Lord revealed more of the plan for my life and the direction of ministry to me. Then one day while I was in prayer, the Lord spoke a word and directed me to turn to the Book of Exodus 14:13: *"And Moses said unto the people, Fear ye not, stand still, and see the salvation of the Lord, which He will show to you today: for the Egyptians whom ye have seen today, ye shall see them again no more forever."* It was the confirmation I needed. Because in life and our Christian walk, there are things we must endure for the cause of Christ. However, some things go beyond God's expectation. I knew He was releasing me from that relationship and ensuring me He would be the covering I needed and He would do the mending and healing needed to move me to the next phase of ministry. Given all of His blessed assurance, I moved on.

Fourteen

My Commitment To The Whosoevers

"So the last shall be first, and the first shall be last. Many shall be called, but few chosen." —Matthew 20:16

As I reflect on this incredible journey as a pastor and in my dedicated service to God, it never ceases to amaze me how wonderfully the Lord operates. God's infinite wisdom is so profound it transcends dimensions and our abilities to comprehend. He is so amazing. I stopped trying to figure Him out many years ago. Instead, I just operate on faith and obedience and watch Him work. Sometimes in our arrogance we fool ourselves into thinking we know God's modus operandi, however, He starts out one way and ends up another leaving us completely baffled. The remarkable thing is that He always ends up exactly where He is supposed to be. Plain and simple, this is His world and we are just living in it. He is God and He can do whatever He wants. King David made it crystal clear when He penned the *24th Psalm*: *"The earth is the*

Lord's and the fullness thereof; the world, and they that dwell therein." —*Psalm 24:1*. God controls everything; therefore, He has liberty to move however He sees fit. God has a divine purpose, strategic assignment and a predetermined plan for the lives of His people.

Our destiny is wrapped up in His will and our success is contingent upon His favor. In the Book of *Jeremiah 29:11*, the Lord states: *"For I know the plans I have for you declares the Lord, plans to prosper you, not to harm you, plans to give you a hope and a future."* In His Master Plan, He knows what we need before we ask. Given that premise, it is extremely critical that you not only know but hear the voice of the Lord.

Consequently, if you are not careful, you may fall prey to the enemy's attempts to imitate the Lord. If we are not spiritually mindful, some things that on the surface make complete sense in theory, will hinder our growth and could lead us astray. In the first Book of Corinthians, the Word of God states: *"For God is not the author of confusion, but of peace, as in all churches of the saints."* —*1 Corinthians 14:33*. Satan is the author of confusion; therefore, if he can mix you up and have your focus in several directions, you will fail to accomplish your goals and God-given assignment. You will become the proverbial cat chasing his tail. Sometimes multi-tasking turns to, in the end, a whole lot of nothing. Lack of focus and singleness of purpose is a recipe for failure in any Kingdom work. The Bible lets us know that, *"A double minded man is unstable in all his ways."* —*James 1:8*. Therefore, understanding and implementing your vision takes serious discipline and attention to detail. When the Lord spoke, I listened and I obeyed. I learned at a very early age obedience is better than sacrifice; and regardless of what I think and feel, always defer to His will. As a result, when the Lord spoke halfway through my post as pastor and let me know He was doing a new thing in the ministry I said, "Yes, Lord, *Thy will be done and thy Kingdom come.*" Shortly afterwards, He spoke a word concerning a change in the ministry.

One evening during our church school service, the Lord moved in an unusual way. It was around that same time we were experiencing a growth spurt in the ministry. This growth surge was atypical. **By that I** mean, God has always added to the church such as should be saved. Notwithstanding, this growth spurt represented a new genre of people. An unusual cadre of folks, who had never before had any real religious experiences, was joining the church in significant numbers. In the past, much of our growth had derived from what are sometimes referred to as "church hoppers" or "church transplants." These groups were primarily made up of people who were unhappy or unsatisfied for various reasons in their previous ministry. Quite frankly, in some circles that terminology could be perceived as a negative connotation, but in no means is that my intent. Everyone has value in the Kingdom.

This new sect expressed an extraordinary determination in their eyes and an insatiable hunger in their spirit. They had an unquenchable thirst for knowledge and direction. They were the new babes in Christ, delicate flowers ready to blossom. Well, about halfway through the church school lesson, a topic came up which touched several people and caused them to share their experiences. The lesson was dealing with deliverance. This lesson must have really hit home to some of the new converts because they talked about the habits and situations from which God had delivered them. One sister talked about a several year addiction to crack cocaine that nearly took her life. She went into grave detail about the ugly demon stranglehold that the drugs had on her. She talked candidly about selling her body for the drugs, and her story hit me to my core — both as a woman and a pastor. I was grateful to God for never having to experience such a horror, but I was empathetic to the sister's struggle. I couldn't show her how much it shook me up, so I just prayed for her as she spoke.

Regularly I say, we never know the struggles that each other face and we all have a story. As her testimony continued, other class attendants sporadically thanked the Lord and praised Him for delivering the sister. It was a powerful and moving account of the sister's experiences. As soon as she finished, another sister testified to the goodness of God. She spoke of her addiction to heroin and the awful things she had to do and how the drug almost destroyed her life. Then one of the new brothers spoke and shared about being delivered from gambling and alcohol abuse. Before I knew it, people just spilt their hearts, speaking passionately about where the Lord had brought them. Collectively, we praised the Lord for all of our victories. I was flabbergasted as I stood in amazement. I searched the crowd and saw others appeared to be as moved as I was; many were the older or more seasoned saints. Mostly, we had been in church our whole lives and had never really been exposed to these things. However, more and more as I get older, I am finding out these seasoned saints had more knowledge then they let on. In the midst of this outpouring, the Lord began to speak about the move and mission of the ministry. He informed me these were the people He would be sending for healing, deliverance and instruction. These were the souls He was entrusting to me, the "Whosoevers." We would be a ministry of the whosoevers. The whosoevers were a group of people that included the lost, the downtrodden and societal outcasts. I had been asking the Lord to fill the church, and He let me know that our church was strategically positioned before the foundation of the world to do this job. Additionally, He let me know that there were thousands of whosoevers living in the community waiting for refuge, looking for deliverance, anxious to be led into the church. In our ministry mission statement, we define ourselves as a spiritual hospital for the sick and a soul-saving station. It was time to take our service up another level and go into the highways and hedges and compel those whosoevers to come.

  The days of church as usual were over. The days of trying to emulate other ministries were over. We were unique and predestined to do Kingdom work. No longer would we seek approval from others or follow some superficial organizational protocols. We had a bigger mandate that superseded church growth by shifting our focus to Kingdom advancement.

The enthusiasm of the whosoevers put a smile on my face and gave me a level of encouragement that ignited a rebirth in me and fueled a movement yet on the rise in our ministry. The whosoevers changed the game. They were hungry, natural and raw. They were sincere people who had a thirst for the Lord. They had just come into relationship with God, and it was my responsibility to teach them how to develop a relationship with the Lord. They had good hearts and were teachable and moldable, open to learning about God and how He operates. Here was a group of gung-ho individuals who were eager and ready to spread the word to their families and friends. They were also ready to help build the ministry. These new babes had an incredible zeal that more than compensated for their lack of knowledge. The whosoevers came to God with expectation and most often free of motives. Ecstatic to have been saved from the mess that enthralled them, and the horrible pit they had been rescued from, made them so grateful. Soon I understood what God was doing. Truthfully, on some levels church had become regular. I mean I never lost my hunger, thirst and desire for the Lord; but collectively, we had become comfortable with the worship process. It was routine and structured, sprinkled with sporadic outpourings of the Holy Spirit. Why weren't we looking for miracles every time the doors open? Many of the saints were set in their ways and fine with the week-in-week-out service. Some people wanted change and wanted to be bigger; but not willing to make the sacrifices to make it happen, instead content in reminiscing about the good ole days.

Although some practiced revisionist history, the record can show that in the so-called good ole days they murmured and complained. Sadly, some are still wandering in the proverbial wilderness, stuck in obscurity. I knew I had to provide a strong covering and special attention to these new saints to ensure that they were not negatively influenced by bitterness and naysayers. God began to strengthen me in my weak areas. He gave me a new level of holy boldness.

For the majority of my life I avoided confrontation and resisted strife. God gave me a new level of discernment. I conducted self-examination, and I also reviewed my service to the membership. I was real about everything. I reflected on the people I poured into, and the moment I did something contrary to their liking, they criticized me. I put them on notice that our ministry was going to the next level with or without them. God showed me it was time for all of us to move to a new level of maturity. We had people coming in who had no previous church history, the whosoevers, and we, the church family, had to be ready to receive them. God knew we had the potential to carry out the mission, but it was my responsibility to prepare the people. I had to demand more from the saints and broaden their horizons. It was up to me to filter out the noise and chatter through intense prayer. I had to prepare the church for what God was doing.

First, I had to define the whosoevers to Little Zion. They had to see how valuable every soul was to the Kingdom. They had to understand that blue hair, the transgendered, face piercing and recovering drug addicts would not be the exception but rather the norm. God had entrusted to us a huge assignment that was not to be treated lightly. We needed to rise to the challenge. We had been so blessed by God. It was time to step up to the plate and explore new territory.

I reminded the saints of the Word in Luke that stated: *"But the one who does not know and does things deserving punishment will be beaten with few blows. From everyone who has been given much, much will be demanded; and from the one who has been entrusted with much, much more will be asked."* — *Luke 12:48*. It was our duty to serve and mentor the new saints. Also, I know the Word of God is clear when it states: *"Knowing that whatsoever good thing any man doeth, the same shall he receive of the Lord, whether he be bond or free."* —*Ephesians 6:8*

The older saints would benefit from their new-formed relationships as much as the whosoevers would benefit from us. As we encouraged our new brothers and sisters, we would be encouraged. All new babes in Christ are fragile and need to be handled with care. I had to spend time with the whosoevers, explaining to them what salvation was about. It was my responsibility to let them know that it was more than just joining a church and giving their lives to God. It was a transformation process that had to take place. I was careful to let them know that salvation is not an escape from prior commitments and consequences. I had to be real with them. God may have forgiven them of their wrongdoings, but there were natural consequences they may still have to face. My main goal was to teach them correctly and reteach what some may have learned in error, and let them know that because you gave your life doesn't mean you will not experience adversity, trials and tribulations. Sometimes zealous people, new in Christ, witness to others setting up false expectations. Sometimes bad information is worse than no information. My goal is to thoroughly equip the saints for their walk of salvation. Another responsibility is to make perfectly clear to these new converts they were under the influence of the adversary until they gave their lives to God, so now the enemy will really come after them and attack. Knowledge is power, especially in the Kingdom. In the Book of Hosea, the Lord talks about how, *"His people perish because of lack of knowledge."* — *Hosea 4:6*

When I adjusted my spiritual lenses and looked deep into the condition of the world and the church, my spirit was troubled. We had developed clicks, factions and even a class system within the confines of ministry. We, the ones who professed unlimited power and potential, had placed some new expectations of the Kingdom in a box. We placed low expectations on church work allowing the "that will do" spirit to creep into the church. People stood in lines for miracle healings and financial blessings but had not been confronted about their lives of sin and iniquity. People prayed for financial blessings and sowed seeds, expecting a harvest, but sadly some were corrupted. We attempted to do major work for God, but the Scripture is clear: *"Except the Lord build the house, they labour in vain that build it: except the Lord keep the city, the watchman waketh but in vain." —Psalm 127:1.* We had to work within God's plan, as opposed to God working within our plan. Some of the new people who had joined the ministry: the ones with the blue and pink hair, the ones with the piercings and the tattoos, those who were once streetwalkers, drug addicts, felons and what the world called dregs of society with all their issues and baggage, in the final analysis were really no different than me. We are all God's children.

Fifteen

Transforming Churchgoers To Kingdom Members

"Therefore, I urge you, brothers, in view of God's mercy, to offer your bodies as living sacrifices, holy and pleasing to God—this is your spiritual act of worship. Do not conform any longer to the pattern of this world, but be transformed by the renewing of your mind. Then you can test and approve what God's will is—his good, pleasing and perfect will." —Romans 12:1-2

The time had come for us to make a paradigm change. As we moved to the next level and began to make changes in our natural lives, we also had to make spiritual changes. One of the most difficult things for all people is change; but when dealing with religion, the sensitivity is heightened 100 fold. Most are resistant and the rest are hesitant, skeptical and uneasy about the unknown. Continuing with what you know is safe and comfortable. But what I soon realized in serving the Lord is that comfortable is not a characteristic of believers. We were not saved to be comfortable, but saved to serve. Part of our church philosophy was our belief that we were created to love, serve and obey God. I knew to serve God in the capacity we were called would be the result of extreme measures. It would require creative persuasion and even greater prayer. This was more than calling for a shut-in; we are talking about a complete transformation. We were looking to move a group of people from that safe, comfortable box to a strange, vulnerable place. If not done correctly, it could be tantamount to Sisyphus pushing that rock up the hill. For many people attending church routinely on Sundays, abstaining from foul language and resisting fornication and adultery made them feel comfortable and safe with their salvation; comfortable, with the assumption they are different or even special.

The Word of God says we are peculiar but not special. He even advised to watch how highly we think of ourselves. Salvation is much more than a few rituals wrapped with morals. Our value to the Kingdom of God requires lots more than we were doing. Truly we are not doing Kingdom work when the souls of saints on either side of us are on the crescendo of hell's door. If people can shout and dance off their fatal flaws and remain comfortable, then we must make an atmosphere change.

Every ministry committed to working and doing the will of God and seeking to reach the lost will confront rebellion from within and indirection from without. There is no such thing as a perfect church or perfect people. Many of the character flaws people have before they get saved and join a church, they still possess after their conversion. When and/or if the right sets of circumstances occur, those old flaws will resurface. If you were a fighter before you got saved, you don't forget how to fight. If you used vulgar language, you still remember those words. When God gives you an assignment, first you have to make the commitment to follow through at all cost. Your commitment to fulfill the assignment could cause the loss of friends and family. Granted you are pleasing God and therefore it is worth it. *"And the Lord answered me, and said, Write the vision, and make it plain upon tables, that he may run that readeth it."* —Habakkuk 2:2

It is incumbent upon you to clarify your vision. Leave no room for ambiguity. Those with you know that you will sacrifice all to make that dream a reality. In addition, they must believe that you are qualified to make it happen. The Spirit of the Lord revealed the vision for my ministry and made it as clear as day. It took a while to share my vision with the saints. I don't know why, maybe because it was partly that I didn't feel they were totally with me in my role as pastor; partly, because I was not emotionally prepared to tackle their criticism; and partly because many were so set in their ways, routines and traditional way we operated church. Many didn't want to be led out of the box and were comfortable churching and going home. But I wanted to take the city for the Kingdom, and I had Malcolm X bravado, whereas I was ready to do it by any Godly means necessary.

I had a three-pronged approach to transform our community. All I needed was my church family to get behind me. But anything worth doing requires passion, discipline and a singleness of purpose. Nehemiah had Sandballot and Tobiah. When he sought to rebuild the walls of the city, they were displeased with the progress and sought to stop it. Joseph had to deal with his brothers who plotted his demise and sold him into slavery. The Word of God is clear about that spirit of rebellion which declares: *"For rebellion is as the sin of witchcraft, and stubbornness is as iniquity and idolatry. Because thou hast rejected the word of the Lord, He hath also rejected thee from being king." —1 Samuel 15:23.*

Being cognizant that the act of rebellion within the ministry is demonic, we must confront it. Some rebellion is disguised with good intention and proposed information seeking. Some of it is practiced through passive aggressive acts. Prayer, our key weapon, will help us. But in addition, we must confront and expose. Troublemakers do their best work in the shadows and undercover. Some people are set in their ways and the way they are used to doing things. While change is difficult and requires an open mind, those resistant must be encouraged to process their feelings and bring them to the Lord in prayer. But in the final analysis, even delayed obedience is rebellion. Each ministry has one head, and it is up to the head to take their instructions from God and those who are subordinate to follow with love, passion and conviction, otherwise move on. Sadly, many ministries are so concerned with the size of their membership rolls they allow talented and resourceful members to get away with certain things that should not be allowed.

Pastors constantly face factions from within that want to dictate what they feel the church should do or in which direction they feel the church should go. If we let down God's standards for larger offerings and greater exposure, we are only dooming ourselves.

Sixteen

The Lord Will Give You A Name Change

He said: "Your name shall no longer be Jacob, but Israel; for you have striven with God and with men and have prevailed."
—Genesis 32:28

Roughly about 15 years ago the Lord spoke concerning the name change of our ministry. Throughout your service and commitment to God, at some point you will get a name change. The more you seek God, the more your life is transformed. That transformation turns you into a new creation. The journey starts with the acceptance of the Lord, but as Kingdom members, only our commencement. The newly-formed relationship we establish with Christ is a starting point to advancing the Kingdom. He let me know that we were entering a new era and it was time to change our name from Little Zion Church to Greater Zion Church. Names are important; they define and identify who you are. In the Book of Isaiah, it states: *"The nations shall see your righteousness, and all the kings your glory, and you shall be called by a new name that the mouth of the Lord will give."* —*Isaiah 62:2.* We were entering a new phase of ministry and we were endeavoring to do greater things, so the new name was fitting. For a long period, I was focused on trying to maintain the ministry my father started. I felt like in doing so I was honoring his memory and on some level, I was satisfied with the small, steady incline. However, deep inside I knew God had bigger things in store for the ministry.

I often reflected on the scripture, *"That some plant, others water, but God gives the increase."* —*1 Corinthians 3:6.* God had been increasing the ministry and giving us favor in the community. He had expanded our sphere of influence and opened doors that had once been closed. In addition, we developed relationships with state and local agencies that enabled us to carry out our vision. Much like God did with Jabez, He enlarged our territory. When we honed down our focus on Kingdom building as opposed to church growth, we began to clearly see the majesty of the Lord's work. While we continued to work on and develop the vision, the Lord continued to open doors that no man could close and close doors that no man could open.

If I had a dollar for all the times I was told that I couldn't lead, I would have enough money to build a brand new church. Countless people told me that I couldn't do it. They told me I wasn't qualified and, in fact, my gender disqualified me. Additionally, things were said like it was a "man's job" and I needed to sit under a man and support his work. They told me how "God operates in order" and the natural order was for man to lead. Contrary to the popular belief of some, I do believe the man is the head of the family and household. And when my husband was alive, I respected and honored him in his role. He was man enough to honor me in my role as the pastor of our church. My role didn't affect or undermine his manhood. Unfortunately, my role did bruise the egos and challenge the manhood of others. Some told me I wasn't strong enough and I didn't have a heart for the people because I was selfish and self-centered. They said everything negative they could think of. But, yet 25 years later I stand, proclaiming the Word of the Lord.

For the first five years of leadership, I went through pure hell. I suffered attacks and attempts to kill my influence from outside and inside the four walls of my church that even included family members who doubted me. I mean some folks really put me through the ringer. In their minds, they just knew I wouldn't make it. Some of those same folks who said, "Give her six months and that church will close up" are no longer around to see the beautiful handiwork of the Lord. Some have gone on to be with the Lord, some have closed the doors to their churches and some, while still pastoring churches, dwell in inconspicuousness. There were times during that period when I thought about giving up. I found myself telling the Lord I couldn't do it. "But thanks be to God," the Lord made a way for me. He remained faithful unto me. Be advised, He will remain faithful to you even when we are unfaithful to Him. Through His faithfulness to me, He also gave me favor.

He opened the hearts and minds of men and women. He moved the obstacles that sat in the midst. I'm so grateful for the Lord for all He has done in my life. As I began a new chapter of my life and ministry, it's my prayer and hope that the new group of leaders chosen by God, some of whom may feel they don't meet the criteria, step into their Godly assignment. The harvest is plenteous but the laborers are few. But pray you to the God of the harvest that He make your feet like hinds feet and He make you to walk upon the high places.

God has a help wanted sign blinking brightly from the clouds of Glory. He wants you to dare to be the leader He has called you to be and trust that He we will equip you with all you need. He has "Great Commission" positions that must be filled before His triumphant return. He is looking for sold out, Kingdom-minded people who are willing to advance His work. He is looking for the whosoever's; those who were once blinded by sin and despair but now have come into the knowledge of Him; those with a new life, a new vision, and a new relationship with Christ; those who are no longer bound by their past and failures. I challenge all that have been called to do anything in this life to push beyond the perils that would attempt to hinder you. No man, no circumstance or situation can stop that which God has ordained.

My prayers are that God prosper and strengthen you in every area of your life. Be willing to lead, but be willing to serve first, and once you master serving, God will make you a leader in His Kingdom.